INVADING SECULAR SPACE

"Though clearly describing the pathetic condition of much of the church in the Western world, Robinson and Smith are neither cynical nor pessimistic. Neither is their challenge just another fad method or strategy to be tried and soon forgotten. Rather, it is a powerful reminder of what church really was intended to be.

"When this book is widely read and taken seriously, the church of the West will accelerate its long road back to 'the creation of healthy communities of believers impacting the world around them', to quote from this excellent work."

Dr. James H Montgomery,
Founder and Chairman of Dawn Ministries

"This book is inspiring, refreshing, transformational, frightening, but essential reading for all Christian leaders who have the desire, courage and faith to see a transformed church impacting the world. I have waited a long time for such a book, and welcome the wisdom, insight and practicality that *Invading Secular Space* offers to me as a leader.

"The writers cut to the heart of the purpose of the church, to give us refreshing foundations for a new day. They present, through history, biblical principle and practical experience, a compelling and essential challenge to a faltering and desperate Western church. Most readers will experience a paradigm change in the way they view and understand the function of church in a post-modern world.

"I believe this book could become a 'classic' on the journey to a relevant church in today's society."

Paul C Weaver,
General Superintendent of Assemblies of God
in Great Britain and Ireland

"This is one of the most timely books regarding the future of Christ's people in the Western world. Well researched, with some amazing statistics, huge challenges, great insights and bags of hope.

Every leader should read this book to find a way forward, reverse the depressing trends and engage with society for the purpose of transformation."

Gerald Coates,
speaker, author, broadcaster, and leader of the
Pioneer network of churches

"*Invading Secular Space* presents a refreshing and provocative insight into how our faith once captured the imagination of the West – and how it could happen again. The authors' urgent insistence on a new kind of leadership for a new culture makes considerable sense. Every church leader in the post-Christian West needs to grapple with these issues – on their knees."

Dr Luis Palau,
international evangelist and author

"I thank God for the passion and practical wisdom in this book. Here are some really useable suggestions for the tough business of making a significant impact on a secular world."

Rev. Stephen Gaukroger,
author and Pastor of Gold Hill Baptist Church, Bucks, UK

"Robinson and Smith focus on the most urgent paradigm shift for the UK church – empowering church leadership to release a movement of disciples ready to transform the secular space within which they are dispersed. Their contribution is both strategic and timely"

Rev. John S Smith,
UK Director, Evangelical Alliance

Invading Secular Space

Strategies for Tomorrow's Church

MARTIN ROBINSON
and
DWIGHT SMITH

MONARCH
BOOKS

Oxford, UK & Grand Rapids, Michigan, USA

First published in the UK in 2003 by Monarch Books,
(a publishing imprint of Lion Hudson plc),
Mayfield House, 256 Banbury Road, Oxford OX2 7DH
Tel: +44 (0) 1865 302750 Fax: +44 (0) 1865 302757
Email: monarch@lionhudson.com
www.lionhudson.com

Reprinted 2005.

Distributed by:
UK: Marston Book Services Ltd, PO Box 269,
Abingdon, Oxon OX14 4YN;
USA: Kregel Publications, PO Box 2607
Grand Rapids, Michigan 49501.

ISBN 1 85424 640 2 (UK)
0 8254 6050 6 (USA)

British Library Cataloguing Data
A catalogue record for this book is available
from the British Library.

Book design and production for the publishers by
Bookprint Creative Services
P.O. Box 827, BN21 3YJ, England.
Printed in Great Britain.

CONTENTS

DEDICATION

To our fathers,
both of whom enabled us
to catch the spirit of mission
long before we learned about it
from books.

ACKNOWLEDGEMENTS

There are a host of people who have helped to make *Invading Secular Space* a reality, and have shared their ideas and aspirations with us. To one and all, our heartfelt appreciation.

Particular thanks go to:

Kevin Popely, without whose persistence and energy the book would never have been written;

Donald McGavran, whose writings proved formative for us both;

The Rt Rev. Mike Hill, Bishop of Bristol, whose enthusiastic support (and foreword) have meant a great deal;

Paul Weaver, General Superintendent of the Assemblies of God, whose encouragement and backing at crucial stages meant more than we can easily express;

Various leaders and church planters within networks around the world, whose example inspired us;

Above all, our long-suffering wives, of whose commitment and patience we have taken far too much advantage.

FOREWORD

BY THE RT REV. MIKE HILL,

BISHOP OF BRISTOL

It is now almost 100 years since the Anglican missionary pioneer, Roland Allen, began to dream of creating a church that would spontaneously expand. The principles that he espoused have now become actual practice in many of the rapidly-expanding churches in Africa, Asia and Latin America. Missiologists talk about these areas of Christian growth as the "Christian South" (even though much of the Asian growth is – strictly speaking – in the Northern hemisphere). The Christian South is increasingly shaping the future of the world church.

Roland Allen was committed to working for the health of the church in the Christian South, and he was also very concerned about the state of the church in the Northern hemisphere. He resigned as vicar of his church in Chalfont St Peter because he could no longer turn a blind eye to the lack of real Christian belief and practice within his own congregation.

Many of the issues that Roland Allen grappled with then have at last come to be taken seriously by the churches in

Europe and North America. Martin Robinson and Dwight Smith are colleagues and friends who are wrestling with these issues. They have brought to bear fresh insights and rigorous thought that will enable church leaders to re-imagine both mission and the shape of the church.

They make their contribution at a timely moment. Some have already given up on the church, believing that even the ability of the church to renew itself is in serious question. But others, such as the sociologist Grace Davie in her helpful book, *Europe – the Exceptional Case*, make a strong case that the church in Europe is actually standing at a moment of great opportunity. She notes that it is the church from the Christian South that is most likely to represent the future for the church in the West.

I belong to that band of optimists that sees the difficulties that the church faces very clearly indeed but still believes that the church is capable of renewal and growth. Such a path will not be easy. It is not enough simply to streamline structures or piously wait for revival. Our engagement with mission and with change needs to be strategic and creative.

The contribution of *Invading Secular Space* is that it offers hard-pressed church leaders imaginative insights as to what needs to be done and why such changes are necessary, as well as a practical indication of how we might tackle the task. If the contents of this book are taken seriously, it may well become a truly landmark publication.

+ Michael Bristol
September, 2003

PREFACE

One of the great passions of both authors of this book is church planting. Martin Robinson has been a church planter, has published at least two books on church planting, and has taught seminars on church planting. Dwight Smith has also been a church planter, was co-founder with Jim Montgomery of Dawn ministries, and has founded a church planting organisation, Saturation Church Planting International (SCPI). In addition, Dwight has encouraged and mentored church planters in many nations.

This book began as a manuscript that reflected that joint passion for church planting. However, because the context is that of the Western world, it was not long before we began to see that we could not say much about church planting without talking a good deal more about leadership. By the time the publisher was approached, this was going to be a book on leadership.

The planning process for the book was not very far advanced before we realised that we could not talk about leadership without talking about the nature and purpose of the church. More than that we could not talk about the church and its mission without addressing at least something of the present context of the Western church and the mission field in which it is set.

That mission field has been dominated over the last several hundred years by the framework of the Enlightenment which constantly seeks to separate the sacred and secular realms, consigning the sacred to the realm of the private and so the unimportant. From a Christian point of view, there can never be two worlds but only God's world. The nature of the relationship between sacred and secular could encompass a book by itself.[1] Suffice it to say that there has been a tendency for Christians to want to invite others into sacred space – sometimes seeker-friendly sacred space. Increasingly, Christians have come to see that mission requires us to grapple in some way with secular space.

The original meaning of secular was simply that which relates to this present age as compared with matters of eternity. For Christians, the event of Jesus Christ means that eternity has come crashing into the present or the secular age. The incarnation was remarkable precisely because God in Christ invaded secular space. At the crucifixion, the curtain in the temple was torn and we are left with the sense that God can never be contained and encountered only in the holy of holies. God is out of the temple and at work in his world.

The structure of the book reflects something of the way in which the authors have been driven to address ever more primary issues. It begins with the missionary context of the church and moves towards a discussion of the nature and purpose of the church. Out of that flows an extended reflection on the nature of leadership and its intended outcomes. The final two chapters address both church planting and the consequent people movement that church planting on a significant scale hopefully produces.

Martin Robinson made a larger contribution to the first few chapters of the book and Dwight Smith a more significant contribution to some of the later chapters. Some other chapters flowed from a wholehearted collaboration. Whichever author initiated a particular chapter, the other author offered significant editorial comment, but the styles of the respective authors should become fairly obvious to the reader.

It is our hope that this book will be followed by other books that pick up themes which are introduced here and which will be extended in a variety of other ways. Dwight Smith hopes to publish a book entirely on leadership, and Martin Robinson is currently working on a book that considers the issue of societal transformation in more detail.

NOTES

1. For a discussion on the relationship between the sacred and secular, the meaning of Christendom and the place of mission, see Oliver O'Donovan, *The Desire of the Nations: Rediscovering the Roots of Political Theology*, Cambridge University Press, 1996, especially chapter seven.

CHAPTER ONE

WHERE HAVE ALL THE PEOPLE GONE?

This book begins with some fundamental convictions. First, that the church is called to share in the mission of God. Second, despite its weaknesses and manifest failures the church continues to occupy a central position in the intention of God for his world. Third, that the church in the Western world finds itself in deep crisis. Fourth, that however profound that crisis might be, the church is called to rediscover its life and witness. Fifth, that the re-imaging of the church can only take place around the centrality of its call to mission. Sixth, the church has encountered such radical challenges in the past. Seventh, that it is possible for the church to be recast to meet the challenges of our age, and that even now signs of the future church can be detected by those with eyes to see.

Those with a love for church history will be very aware how tenuous the life of the church has been on occasion. David Bosch, in his magisterial work, *Transforming Mission*,[1] borrows from Hans Küng and outlines six major paradigms in the history of the church in the West. He makes the telling point that the transition from one paradigm to the next has come as a consequence of and a response to situations of profound theological, missiological and cultural challenge. In the midst of the transition, few, if any, could see the shape of the church to come. Just as importantly, many who were living in the turmoil were unsure whether the church would survive the crisis then facing it.

One crisis alone makes the point. At the time of the collapse of the Roman Empire, when Roman troops were withdrawn from Britain in the face of invasions by Angles and Saxon peoples, the church in a large part of Britain (the part that became England) faced virtual extinction. The church had to be re-established and the Christian community that reappeared looked dramatically different from the church that had been present during Roman occupation. The church that then existed played a very small part in creating the new church that was to come. The Christians of the time were powerless to deal with the forces that were overwhelming them.

The missionary story of that particular transition from crisis to a new church is a complex matter. One book written by an Irish-American journalist describes an important element in its engaging title – *How the Irish Saved Civilization*.[2] The zeal of the Celtic saints (mainly Irish), together with the work of missionaries from Rome, helped to lay the foundations for European civilisation in the medieval period.

Few commentators doubt that we are living in similarly difficult times. We do not face invasion by conventional armed forces, but we are in a time of profound cultural conflict and change. It is important that we grasp the extent of the crisis. Just how serious is the situation that the church in the Western world faces at the beginning of the third millennium?

THE PRESENT GROWTH AND DECLINE OF CHRISTIANITY

The cardinal had a stark message: "It does seem in our countries in Britain today, especially in England and Wales, that Christianity, as a sort of backdrop to people's lives and moral decisions – and to the government, the social life of the country – has now almost been vanquished."[3] His words were picked up by the popular press and misquoted as meaning that Christianity itself is defeated in Britain. That was not what the cardinal intended to say nor what he actually said. Christianity is not dead in Britain, yet few can question that something is seriously amiss.

It is not just that the statistics reveal an unremitting decline in church membership and attendance. Something more fundamental has been taking place during the second half of the 20th century in Western Europe and arguably in virtually every developed country that has previously seen Christianity as the primary expression of belief in their society.

Yet curiously the difficulties encountered by the church in the West do not reflect the global position of the church. Far from it. The worldwide church has demonstrated astonishing life and vigour in precisely the same period that the Western church has suffered reversal and decline. So how do we assess what happened during the 20th century?

In 1998, BBC television got in early with their review of the 20th century entitled *The People's Century*. Cynics in the press commented that such a title reflected a very optimistic perspective. Some suggested that a more representative experience of the 20th century would have yielded the title "The Dictator's Century". After all, this had been the century of Stalin, Hitler, Mao Tse-Tung, Pol Pot, Pinochet, to name but a few. The experience of democracy has been the reality for a small minority.

I want to suggest that viewed from the perspective of transforming people movements, the 20th century might properly be called "The Christian Century". We are living in the middle of an astonishing time for mission. Latin America, Africa, Eastern Europe and some parts of Asia are witnessing the rapid growth of the church. Each of these stories is itself complex and different but the overall result is that the church has never grown faster, has never before been so widely represented across the globe, has never been as multicultural, has never sent so many missionaries from so many continents to so many nations.

This story of a flourishing church began in the late 18th century, following on from the outbreak of revival and the creation of the modern missionary movement. However, its earlier dependency on Western missions was decisively ended with the emergence of vigorous indigenous churches, notably in the last 30 to 40 years – the years of post-colonial independence.

The church historian, Mark Noll, has claimed that the great achievement of mission in the 19th century was the conversion of North America, that the great missionary achievement of the 20th century has been the conversion of much of Africa south of the Sahara and that the great achievement of mission in the 21st century will be the conversion of many parts of the continent of Asia. That single sentence contains a summary which needs to be unpacked in much more detail, and like many bold statements requires some qualification, but Noll's summary statement points us to a number of astonishing facts.

We can all too easily forget how recent the conversion of North America has been. We frequently make the assumption that Christianity went to America with the Pilgrim Fathers and has been the dominant and constant companion of Americans ever since. Such an assumption overlooks the struggles, divisions and disappointments of early American Christianity, and fails to understand the transforming significance of the vast revival movements of the early and mid-19th century.

Some parts of the United States, for example the north-west, were untouched by those revival movements and have never had a Christian majority. Today, attendance at worship in the state of Washington is more akin to the United Kingdom than to the rest of the United States. Without those 19th century revivals, or people movements, the experience of the whole of the United States would more likely reflect that of Seattle than Cincinnati.

In thinking of Africa, it is all too easy to imagine that it was a continent merely waiting for the Christian faith to arrive. Such a view overlooks the relatively slow progress that Christianity made in the early days of missionary activity. Those early pioneers such as David Livingstone may have been much loved and admired, but the number of actual converts that they won to Christ hardly guaranteed the future of the Christian church in Africa.[4] More crucially, it also overlooks the strength of tribal religions and more critically the steady advance of Islam from its north African, Arab stronghold towards southern Africa. Had Christianity not flourished in 20th century Africa, it is almost certain that Africa would by now be a predominantly Muslim continent.

Christianity in Asia is not advancing at a uniform rate in every land. The Philippines is to date the only nation in Asia where Christians represent the overwhelming majority. However, the gospel has made huge inroads in South Korea, parts of India such as Nagaland, in Singapore and arguably in Indonesia. There are significant Christian minorities in countries as diverse as Japan, Thailand, Vietnam, Nepal, India as a whole, and Malaysia. Perhaps the most surprising story of all is that of Christianity amongst the Chinese, both in mainland China and amongst the Chinese diaspora. No one can yet be sure of the precise situation of Christianity in China. Estimates of the number of Christians vary from the official government figure of 20 million to speculative estimates of 100 million (or nearly 10% of the population). Enthusiastic Chinese Christian leaders speak of their hope that China will be a majority Christian nation by the end of the 21st century.

It is hard to know how accurate such predictions might be, but we can be sure of some facts. Before the communists expelled Christian missionaries in 1949, there were some 3 million Christians in China. That figure seemed to remain constant despite population growth until after the Cultural Revolution of the 1960s. Since that time the church has grown dramatically. It seems likely that the figure of 20 million is far too low even by virtue of the fact that the Bible Societies have printed more than 20 million Bibles in China and have distributed them to Christians (distribution to non-Christians is forbidden). The growth of the Chinese church has a considerable impact on the shape of the world church. It represents one of the largest people movements in the history of Christian missions. If such growth continues throughout the 21st century and the hopes of Chinese leaders are fulfilled, then global Christianity will look far less Western and far more Eastern than it has ever done before.

We live in exciting times for mission. Even in some Muslim lands there seem to be opportunities for the growth of the church that have never existed before. But the global spread of the Christian faith, the confident rejoicing in the progress of the church, comes to a shuddering halt when we examine the state of the church in nearly every Western land.

Despite the fact that most cities in Europe have skylines that still feature church spires and city centres whose roads lead to large and beautiful cathedrals, the situation of the church is worrying and getting worse. It is claimed that less than 1% of the population attends church in Copenhagen and that under 5% of the population attends church in most Scandinavian countries. Even though the figures for church attendance in Catholic southern Europe are not yet as low as for Protestant northern Europe, there is a dramatic drop in attendance which so far shows no sign of slowing. Even in the Catholic Republic of Ireland, the cultural dominance of the Catholic church is being severely challenged with attendance at Mass declining significantly.

It is not just the numerical decline of Christianity in the West that gives cause for concern, even though attendance and membership figures graphically illustrate the problem. The figures illustrate a problem much more serious than the diffi-culty of attracting new members and keeping existing members. Callum Brown, in his book *The Death of Christian Britain*, speaks of a much more decisive break with a Christian past. He suggests that the cycle of the renewal of Christianity was dramatically broken in the 1960s and that a whole genera-tion of Christians abandoned the faith in a way that has been unprecedented in the whole history of the church in the West.

He writes:

> It took several centuries to convert Britain to Christianity, but it has taken less than forty years for the country to forsake it.[5]
> . . . What scholars have imagined is religious decline as a long-term process that has left today's Britons with a residual Christian belief but no churchgoing habit. In all of these cases, Christian decay in Britain has been perceived as a decline without an imagined end. This book imagines the end.[6]

The forsaking of the faith that Brown describes is reflected in a loss in the influence of the church such that Christian values and teaching no longer impact the public life of many Western nations today. Indeed it is possible to argue that there is a deeply ingrained prejudice against Christianity on the part of many policy makers in the public life of the West. Christianity is scorned, derided and ridiculed. It is no longer seen as the inspiration from which we derive a sense of who we are and who we might aspire to be.

Given the extent and seriousness of this decline and rejec-tion, why are church leaders not entirely occupied with asking how such a situation can be reversed? Why is it not the top agenda item for every church council, parish meeting, synod and conference? Three issues emerge.

1. Financial Insulation

The past still bankrolls the present. In much of Western Europe, it is possible for the state churches, which have experienced the biggest declines in attendance, to be insulated from the consequences of decline. The first and most obvious insulation is financial. The church tax, a feature of many northern European lands, is still paid by many who do not attend church. That is because in some unconscious way people still want to be identified with the church, either because it speaks to their sense of being Swedish, or Danish, or because they believe that this is a way of "buying" the attention of the church with regard to the rites of passage – baptism, marriage and burial – or because the church is fondly remembered as part of the community.

The wealth of the church relative to actual attendance means that the views of those who do attend do not have to be considered since their financial contribution is negligible compared to those who do not attend but are only present through their church tax. They are absent, unbelieving but contributing members. Moreover, it is possible for a local church to employ large numbers of people from such income to such an extent that it is possible for the number of staff to exceed the regular lay attendance. I attended just such a church in Denmark – 27 paid staff (part- or full-time), less than 20 in the congregation.

Such an economic distortion can even lead to clergy neglecting their duty. The minister of one state church in Sweden with a Charismatic style of worship and a large congregation told me that some of his fellow clergy in other parishes thought him foolish to work so hard. From their perspective, a large congregation simply produced too much work and since their pay was guaranteed however many people attended, they did not feel a particular strong incentive to extend their working hours. Theirs was a profession more than a passion.

One church leader in Germany told me that the church in

his land is still well treated by the media and that the impression given by media treatment is far better than the actual experience of going to church. That information was somewhat surprising to someone from the United Kingdom where the experience of church is usually better than the impression given by a hostile media. The moderation of the media with regard to the church in some European nations helps to preserve the financial commitment of a population who actually stand in need of evangelisation. It is unlikely that such benevolence will remain forever.

In the United Kingdom, some denominations rely on decline to finance their structures. In very crude terms, non-conformist denominations, which do not have the commitment of the Anglican church to a comprehensive coverage of the nation, are able to sell buildings, using the resources of the past to insulate themselves against the present and so mortgage the future.

2. The Gradual Nature of Decline

Those who conduct research into such matters suggest that the numerical decline of the churches in Europe began 150 years ago and has continued ever since. When decline first began it was hardly noticed, because it was a decline, not of actual membership, but decline as a percentage of a rapidly growing population. The noticeable decline in membership began for many denominations after the First World War. Even then it was gradual and could be explained by social factors, such as the war, which leaders at the time felt were only temporary and would be overcome. Even more confusing for church leaders have been the brief periods when decline has slowed and has even been temporarily reversed. The 1950s looked like one of those periods for the church.

The 1960s and 1970s brought huge decline for nearly every denomination in Europe and although the decline has slowed in recent times, the long-term patterns are clear and unremitting. Living with decline as a long-term constant factor dulls the senses as to its seriousness. Increasingly, observers in the United States are pointing to the late arrival of these same trends to American church life. If nothing changes, the American church may well come to mirror the experiences of the European churches.

3. No one Knows What To Do About the Problem

There is a widespread feeling that no one knows what to do and so it is very hard to worry too much about a problem that afflicts virtually every church when no one is offering any solutions. I would not categorise this as a sense of despair so much as a grasping of what seems to be cold logic.

The absence of a quest for a solution to decline seems to have been amplified, at least in the United Kingdom, by a feeling that numerous solutions had been tried and found wanting. Many of the individual remedies that had been adopted for a time came from the United States but were adopted in the early 1990s in the context of the Decade of Evangelism (or Evangelisation). Willow Creek with its Seeker Service approach, Rich Warren and his Purpose Driven Church, experiences of the Toronto Vineyard Church or Pensacola, came and went.

Eddie Gibbs makes this helpful observation: "Unfortunately, most pastors and church leaders have had no missiological training. Consequently, pastors in North America resort to marketing strategies because many urban and suburban congregations are in competition with each other to position themselves and to gain a larger stake in the religious market."[7] It is essentially the same impulse in the United Kingdom that causes church leaders to look to the United States for market-focussed solutions without necessarily being aware of the underlying driving force.

To those market-focussed American solutions were added some uniquely British initiatives such as Reinhard Bonnke's distribution programme and the Jesus In Me formula which began in the Pentecostal churches. All of these experiences could be placed in the longer-term context of the Charismatic Movement with its promise of power for the church, the Evangelism Explosion methodology, Church Growth thinking and many more. The overall impact seems to have been to reduce many church leaders to the conclusion, "I don't want to hear about any other initiative for growth – I've tried them all and none of them have worked. All I want to do now is pray and hope that the church doesn't decline too much before I retire." The notion that decline is everyone's problem somehow acts to stop it being anyone's problem in particular.

If many of the solutions tried by congregations in Europe came originally from the United States, is there any evidence that these approaches work better in an American climate compared with a European one? To the European eye, church life in North America is incomparably healthier than anything available in Europe. The percentage of the population in church on the average Sunday is about the same as it was in late Victorian England.

Figures from Gallup demonstrate that church attendance in the United States of America as a percentage of the population has remained constant for many decades. Some researchers present a slightly more pessimistic view than this. However, it is true that mega- and even metachurches abound, money for missions seems plentiful by comparison with the United Kingdom, gifted individuals still train for the ministry, and Christian institutions, especially in the field of education, seem to flourish. Compared with Europe, it does not seem particularly hard to build congregational life. The average American seems to be more intrinsically religious in outlook as compared with a more obviously secularised European.

But many astute observers recognise that not all is well with

American church life. George Barna writes in his book *The Second Coming of the Church*: "I believe the church in America has no more than five years – perhaps even less – to turn itself around and begin to affect the culture, rather than be affected by it."[8]

Jack Dennison from CitiReach International suggests that perhaps 80% of the 375,000 churches are in decline, or plateaued primarily because they have lost their connection with and their ability to identify with and influence the people and culture around them. Eddie Gibbs cites the researcher Mike Regele of Percept Group Inc as saying, "The institutional church in America will look very different 25 years from now, and several denominations may no longer exist."[9]

Three issues point to a deeper malaise. First, as compared with the situation at the beginning of the 20th century, Christianity is gradually becoming confined to the cultural margins of society. In 1900, the New York missionary convention commanded a mainstream position in society. Not only did thousands of ordinary Americans attend this event, but so too did leaders from the world of politics, education and industry. A missionary convention not only caught the public imagination but it also made headlines in the secular media. A Christian vision of society and the world stood at the centre of the popular imagination in terms of what it meant to be American.

Gradually, especially since the 1960s, the Christian church has been driven to the sidelines in terms of the cultural mainstream. Whether it be images driven from Hollywood, music generated in the ghettos of American cities, corporate training courses that draw from New Age thinking or a gradual exclusion from the daily life of the public school system, American Christians have been increasingly driven to create their own subculture as compared with their earlier exercise of a dynamic influence over mainstream culture. It is as if American Christianity never recovered from the shock of its symbolic defeat during the Scopes trials of the 1920s.

It can certainly be argued that the social significance of Christianity was maintained for some decades by a liberal form of the faith which sought to accommodate the faith to an increasingly secular outlook. But such marriages are intensely dangerous when the secular partner, sensing that this was always a contrived marriage of two unequal partners, seeks a divorce. In more recent years, Evangelical Christians have attempted a second marital arrangement, portraying Christianity as a more virtuous element of a consumerist story. The consumption of Jesus is presented as a more fulfilling way to live the American dream, but not as a fundamental challenge to the idea of the good life configured as "more of everything".

Second, it is becoming clear that if Christianity now operates on the margins of American cultural life, it is increasingly difficult to persuade those who are under 30 to remain part of such a subculture. Compared with Europe, the American church has many young people in its congregations. Compared with the situation a generation ago, it is clear that the church in America is finding it increasingly difficult to transmit a Christian narrative to the coming generations. Congregations in North America are growing older.

Third, American church life has been heavily dependent on programmes at a time when programmes are increasingly under suspicion. As compared with Europe, Americans are notable for their capacity to join social organisations, everything from bowling groups to town guilds, but there are some powerful indicators which suggest that this "joining" feature of American life is undergoing change. The academic Robert Putnam captured this trend in the title of his book, *Bowling Alone*.[10] In the midst of such change, programme-oriented churches are beginning to struggle to maintain institutional life.

The North American researcher, Loren Mead, in his book *Transforming Congregations for the Future*, makes the follow-

ing crucial observations. He points out that the storm facing
churches in America is so serious that it marks the end of business as usual.[11] Concerning the drop-out in membership and
attendance, he points out "that the most important factor in
the drop-out is not something that the churches are doing or
not doing; it is the character of the culture surrounding the
congregations".[12]

For the church that is used to operating programmes such
information is hugely problematic. Mead states his thesis with
even more clarity. He continues:

> The information is startling and dismaying to church leaders. It
> suggests that the things we know how to do best have little to do
> with who stays or who goes. We know how to develop
> programmes. Apparently the population is not interested in
> programmes. It suggests that the very way we organise ourselves to
> respond to the problem of church drop-outs may have very little
> impact on the people who drop out.
>
> The cultural environment may be more determinative to
> membership losses than the character of what the congregation is
> and does . . .[13]

Does that mean that we can simply blame the nature of the
cultural environment and conclude that we should do nothing?
That is not the lesson that Mead is drawing. He explains that
we are not facing an impossible challenge, merely one that is
different than we had previously imagined:

> In the area of membership losses, we are not dealing with some-
> thing that is responsive to a new program – even a very good
> program. We are engaged in a basic interaction between religious
> institutions and the nature of our social environment. The
> researchers have lifted the problem to a new level of difficulty and
> called us to move beyond our narrow answers to address larger
> issues than we have heretofore had the guts to face.
>
> . . . we do not need a new set of programs. We need churches

with a new consciousness of themselves and their task. The structures we have inherited have shown little capacity for such radical
rethinking of their identity.[14]

Mead is making the point that two critical issues cry out to be
addressed. The first is what he calls the self-consciousness of
the church and its task. We might restate that as the core identity and purpose of the church – its DNA. The second is that
the nature of the interaction between the church and the
culture it seeks to address needs to be rethought. In other
words the church must re-imagine its mission. Part of that re-
imagining concerns our relationship with people who live
entirely in secular space, in this world. It can never be sufficient
to constantly construct programmes designed to pull people
into sacred space, we have to also consider how we might
invade secular space. It is these two issues, the nature of the
church and the nature of its mission, that this book seeks to
explore.

CHANGING MINDS, CHANGING CHURCH

Before we explore these two issues in any depth, it is vital to
point out that past discussions of such matters have tended
to avoid significant analysis of the problem and jump all too
quickly to suggested methodological solutions. A number of
writers have suggested that the tendency to search for methods
or strategies to reverse decline is itself part of our cultural
captivity. The very culture of modernity suggests that for every
problem there must be a simple (or possibly complex – but we
prefer simple) methodological solution. Our technological age
entices us down this obvious but empty road. It is as if our
culture causes us to cry out, "Don't tell me about the problem.
Just give me the solution." Even as I have shared this
thought from public platforms, I can see in the faces of some to
whom I am speaking, and hear in the questions afterwards, the

sentiment which says, "So what's wrong with that?"

What's wrong is that even on its own terms – i.e. it must be good if it works – it doesn't work and it doesn't work because the nature of the problem does not lend itself to such solutions. We have to look deeper. "But," some still object, "some churches are growing. Haven't they discovered something that we can learn from?"

Certainly there are some growing churches across Europe and in North America but with a few notable exceptions, what such churches have actually learned is not how to become significant missionary congregations but how to attract Christians from other churches more effectively than other congregations can. Conversations with the pastors of churches which are perceived to be "successful" congregations reveal all too often that the extent of their evangelistic outreach and missionary impact in the community is all too small, especially in relation to their size. Indeed the pastors of such congregations readily admit that they do not know how to mobilise their people for mission. Many point to their size and perceived success as factors that help to prevent their people from taking mission too seriously. There is sometimes a feeling in the congregations of larger churches that they don't need to engage in much that is mission because the church just grows by attraction, and those that are attracted are already Christians.

Undoubtedly there are some congregations that do succeed in bringing significant numbers of people to Christian faith and commitment and which make an impact on their community. However, it is noticeable how difficult it has been for their efforts to be replicated elsewhere. The principles may be replicable but in practise few manage to successfully reproduce by methodological means alone that which succeeds somewhere else. The transmission of a missionary DNA is more biological than technological. It has more to do with life and vision, with community and authentic lifestyle, than with techniques and

methods alone. Although it is difficult to write about something as intangible as life and vision as compared with the
definable nature of a methodology, the following four areas
indicate the kind of thinking that will be necessary to enter a
new missionary paradigm.

1. Changing our Subliminal Thinking

The secret question on the minds of many leaders is the very
simple issue: "How do I grow my church?" The importance
attached to this subject is revealed every time ministers meet. If
clergy do not know each other, then the initial three questions
are these: first, "What's your name, and where are you from?",
second, "What denomination, stream or churchmanship are
you from?" – in other words, "What is your church like?", and
third, "What size is your church?" A supplementary question
might be: "How are things going?" by which is meant, "Are
you growing or declining?" If the answer indicates that the
church is doing well and growing, then the conversation may
well turn to questions around the theme, "So what are you
doing to produce such growth?"

What leaders want to hear is not the pious response, "I
spend four hours praying every day and God does the rest", to
which most clergy would respond, "Who are you trying to kid
– what are you *really* doing?" They assume and want to know,
what programme(s) such a minister has instituted to produce
these great results. They would also like to know that it does
not cost too much, that they can learn it without too much
difficulty, and that it is relatively easy to implement. The cry of
their hearts is "Give me a quick-fix programme and preferably
one I can easily sell to the leaders of my church and one that
does not stretch next year's budget too seriously".

Such thinking is both understandable and can even be well
intentioned. To want to see one's congregation grow and make
a significant impact on local community life is a laudable but

possibly misplaced sentiment. That secret question, however well intentioned, is the wrong one.

A better question would be: "How can I ignite a movement round here?" That suggests a different starting point. Of course, if one can begin a movement then it is very possible that one's church will grow but the priorities will be very different.

At the beginning of the Jesus Movement, Chuck Smith, the pastor of Calvary Chapel in California, tells the moving story of how his congregation prayed fervently for revival and especially to reach young people with the gospel. They had tried many methods and none had succeeded. When, unexpectedly, a group of people from a hippie lifestyle started to attend the church and began to follow Jesus, Chuck Smith had a hostile response from some in the congregation. When they had prayed for revival (a movement from God), this was not quite what they had in mind. Chuck Smith had to make some choices and he chose to go with the movement that was being ignited. As a consequence his church did grow dramatically but another possibility was that he might have lost his job.

2. Abandoning the Collection and Amusement Impulse

The implied priority behind the question "How can I get my church bigger?" is the notion that the key issue is how to collect and amuse a congregation. All too often, programmes are seen as assisting ministers to collect a congregation and keep them amused rather than as a primary tool of mission.

Another way of thinking about our people is to stop seeing them as programme participants and start seeing them as activists who are yet to be mobilised and trained. Igniting movements happens primarily through the Christians we mobilise in their spheres of influence. Programmes can become useful tools to strengthen and enhance movement making but training our people to be effective in the marketplace or other primary social circles is more important than persuading them to participate in programmes.

Think about the youth in your church. Ask the question, is it better to have great programmes at church that we hope will be attractive to youth in the area or is it better to envision the youth we do know so that they can influence their friends and ignite a movement? Of course, once we have understood the primary importance of mobilising and training our people, then programmes can take their proper place. Programmes are great tools in the hands of mobilised people but they do not have the same impact or value without that primary training and envisioning.

3. Focus on the Raw Material for Movement Making

The primary focus for many ministers is to organise the gathering of Christians. That organising may be around Sunday worship, or it may be around mid-week groups or special events or even church camps. But the primary goal is to think both how to gather people and what to do with them once they are gathered. There is nothing wrong with such gathering activity by itself. However, somewhere along the way we have lost sight of the reason for gathering. At its worst, the idea of gathering together, feeling that we have been well ministered to, and even better, that more and more people are gathering each week, is reason enough for gathering.

The most important goal for ministers is to think through the following:

- How can I help my people to experience intimacy with God?
- How can I help people to encounter the grace of God and speak about it to others?
- How can I help people to discover their giftedness and their call?

- How can I help people to live a lifestyle that speaks of Christ?

In short, if ministers of the gospel are called to proclaim the story, how do we encourage the church to discover how to live the story? If we can succeed in leading our people down such a road then we are on the way to producing a movement as our members begin to spontaneously impact their areas of influence. We may want to use programmes and times of gathering to engage in these issue. How we do it is not as important as actually investing in the raw material for movement making.

4. Presume that God has Gone Ahead of Us

How do we see the world immediately around us? Do we see it as a place of mission which God is already opening up for us or do we see it as a place of immense threat – as the enemy to be overcome? Confidence in God and in the missionary enterprise of the Holy Spirit is basic to movement building.

All across the Western world, at this time, religion is back on the agenda. Spirituality is something that fascinates people. It is not that there is no appetite for spiritual ideas, only a lack of conviction that the church has much to offer. Many indicators signal the extent of the spiritual quest occupying many in the Western world today.

Writing in a new book that describes experiments in the emerging church, Michael Frost and Alan Hirsch point to the Burning Man phenomenon or Black Rock Desert event as the "ultimate postmodern festival" in these words:

Each year, thousands of artists, musicians, bohemians, punks, taggers, rappers and other artistes, or simply interested bystanders, journey into the 107-degree heat of the desert for a festival like none other. There they form a temporary community of people

committed to generosity, environmentalism, celebration, spirituality, and, above all, art. Burning Man has been so successful over
the past five years that it can now be seen to represent those
trends that pose the single greatest challenge to the Christian
church. It dares to offer acceptance, community, an experience
of God, redemption and atonement. In short, it claims to
offer everything that the church has been offering over the
centuries. But many people are finding the transformative power of
Burning Man far and away more effective than anything they find
in church.[15]

For Hirsch and Frost, Burning Man is a challenge to the
church but it is also a sign of longing and searching. A re-
imagined church needs to learn how to address the yearnings
that such a phenomenon represent.

Second, it is not merely the bohemian fringes of society that
are experiencing such longings. Even prestigious business
schools are recognising the place of spirituality as a key factor
in good leadership. The longing for God is acute and
profound. The researcher David Hay, who has worked for
many years on the subject of spirituality, estimates that explicit
interest in spiritual matters approximately doubled amongst
those outside of the church during the decade of the 1990s. His
research tellingly points to the fact that many of those that he
has interviewed have spiritual longings but do not have a
language with which to express those desires. The lack of
language causes them to draw on whatever images or ideas,
from science fiction to yoga, are available to them.

That impression is confirmed by some research which
attempted to discover the values of younger people outside of
the church. Derek Hughes was struck by the extent to which
young people longed to be loved, to have authentic relationships, to experience meaningful community. In fact they tended
to describe their longings in precisely the terms that the
New Testament describes the true nature of the church.

Significantly, when asked, "What would you give to be part of such a community?" they responded, "Almost anything".[16]

The populations of the West are open to spirituality, they yearn for an experience of community that the church would like to offer but has forgotten how to model. What we see before us is not a hopeless cause but an open door for mission. We might very reasonably conclude that the Holy Spirit has been busy preparing the way for the church. In such a situation the church is called to reconsider its core life and purpose.

NOTES

1. David Bosch, *Transforming Mission*, Orbis, 1991, p. 187ff.
2. Thomas Cahill, *How the Irish Saved Civilization: The Untold Story of Ireland's Heroic Role from the Fall of Rome to the Rise of Medieval Europe* (Hinges of History, Vol 1), Doubleday, 1995.
3. Gary Finn, "Pope and new age beliefs 'have killed Christianity'", Special report: religion in the UK, *The Guardian*, 6 September, 2001. See also, Martin Wainwright, "Christianity faces day of judgement", Special report: religion in the UK, *The Guardian*, 7 September, 2001.
4. It has been suggested that Livingstone only ever produced one convert. Towards the end of his life there was a widespread feeling that his ministry had been something of a failure. His rehabilitation as a missionary pioneer and an appreciation of his wider significance have largely taken place since his death.
5. Callum Brown, *The Death of Christian Britain*, Routledge, 2001, p. 1.
6. Ibid., p. 3.
7. Eddie Gibbs and Ian Coffey, *Church Next: Quantum Changes in Christian Ministry*, IVP, 2001, p. 41.
8. George Barna, *The Second Coming of the Church*, Word Publishing, 1998, p. 8.

9. Eddie Gibbs and Ian Coffey, cited above, p. 19.
10. Robert Putnam, *Bowling Alone: The Collapse and Revival of American Community*, Simon and Schuster, 2000.
11. Loren Mead, *Transforming Congregations for the Future*, Alban Institute, 1994, p. ix.
12. Ibid., p. 16.
13. Ibid.
14. Ibid., p. 17.
15. Michael Frost and Alan Hirsch, *The Shaping of Things to Come*, Alban Books, 2003, p. 8.
16. Derek Hughes, unpublished manuscript in the possession of the author.

CHAPTER TWO

WHAT ON EARTH IS THE CHURCH FOR?

The question of the primary purpose of the church is not as straightforward as many would like to imagine. In the mid-1980s the British Council of Churches ran a Lenten Study programme with the title, "What on Earth is the Church For?" Those who participated in that study series reported that many had difficulty in articulating a description of what the church was for. They were not against the church, far from it. They were very committed members, but they just weren't clear about the purpose of the church.

By coincidence, a few days before these pages were written, another small group that I attended revisited that same question of two decades ago – what on earth is the church for? We had some better quality answers on this occasion. Some inevitably focussed on tasks that the church engages in, "hatching, matching and dispatching", while others responded with activities that mattered to them – friendship, fellowship, encouragement, prayer and care. A few offered more theological responses, such as bringing pleasure to God and the worship and praise of God. Others wanted to include elements of the proclamation of the faith. One person recognised that the church has a sociological function in relation to society and in particular, local communities. These were all good responses but the discussion revealed that the question is far from straightforward.

The issue is difficult because in one sense it is not a biblical question. The Bible does not set out to ask or answer such a question in a direct or systematic way. The fact that the Bible does not address the purpose of the church as an integral part of the mission of Jesus has led some to ask whether Jesus ever intended to found the church. Hans Küng, amongst many others, is convinced that Jesus and his immediate followers preached about the kingdom of God and spent no time at all preparing the structure of a new organisation.[1] The significance of the twelve was not because this represented a good size for a discipleship group but specifically because they stood for a renewed Israel. The twelve tribes would be reconstituted in these individuals as a direct sign of the imminence of the kingdom of God. The gradual realisation that the arrival of the kingdom would be delayed forced the believers to deal with the church as a present reality. As one scholar wryly noted, the early Christian community was expecting the kingdom and what came was the church.

Not only did the first Christians not think about the church and what it was for, the Christian thinkers and leaders of the first few centuries hardly dealt with the question either. Their agenda concentrated on the content of the Christian message and not on the vehicle that proclaimed it. As Alister E McGrath puts it:

> Ecclesiology was not a major issue in the early church. The Eastern church showed no awareness of the potential importance of the issue. Most Greek patristic writers of the first five centuries contented themselves with describing the church using recognisably scriptural images, without choosing to probe further.[2]

So, if the New Testament does not focus on the church and its purpose, and if the church of the first few centuries paid scant attention to the issue, should we worry about the question at all? Ironically it was the very success of the mission of the church that first forced Christians to consider the issue of the church, its nature and its mission.

The creeds gradually began to reflect on the nature and purpose of the church. The credal statement, "We believe in one holy, catholic and apostolic Church" highlights the tensions that began to afflict the church. What does it mean to say we believe in the church? The context of the creed suggests that Christians are declaring their belief, not in the church itself as an institution, so much as in its message.[3]

Over time, the church did come to consider the question of its own life and purpose. A good number of church historians believe that it was the coming of Christendom, the establishing of the church as an institution with a defined relationship with the state, that brought such a development. However, even before the church was given a legal existence by Constantine, the very persecutions suffered by the church introduced divisions which caused such questions to be addressed. In particular, the church agonised over the issue of the "lapsed" – those who renounced their faith at times of persecution. What should happen to them once the persecution had ceased and they wished to rejoin the church? It does not take much imagination to see that those who had suffered did not take kindly to the easy readmission to the church of those who had avoided all pain or loss.

Yet to keep people out of the church suggests that church membership, its privileges in terms of the sacraments, and the explicit promise of eternal life, carried value. The church was a valuable social and religious entity bridging this life with the next. In this sense, one does come to believe in the church because of what membership of the church represents and effects.

THE COMING OF CHRISTENDOM

It is nevetheless true that the question of the purpose of the church becomes much more obvious as a question in the context of Christendom. It is important to be clear when we use the somewhat slippery term "Christendom". Some have sought to describe Christendom in purely territorial terms but in reality, the concept carries a much more profound meaning. It points to a particular relationship between state and church which is by no means simple and which is certainly capable of a number of interpretations.

The heart of the relationship centres on the notion that the state (which operates in the secular realm – the here and now) accepts the truth of Christianity and so attempts to base its actions around that truth. The church does not seek to be sidelined to the role of a service agency dispensing valuable religious functions through a priesthood, but rather seeks to remind the secular power of the limits of its power and to infuse its deliberations with an eternal perspective.

In this sense the church is never subject to the state as an obedient servant, but rather the state has come to accept the wisdom of the gospel. The relationship is therefore very complex. In the sense of the power of ideas, of ideology, the state is subject to the church. But in the exercise of power in the sense of physical coercion, the church is always subject to the state. The balance of the equation lies in the preservation of justice.

How did this kind of question arise at all? The experience of the church prior to Constantine ranged from that of a persecuted and hated sect to a tolerated and respected minority religion. But during that immensely difficult period the church was able gradually to win some important victories. The social engagement of the church in helping the poor and the marginalised undoubtedly won the church many friends. As one author has put it:

In cities of growing social divisions, Christianity offered unworldly
equality. It preached, and at its best it practised, love in a world of
widespread brutality.[4]

Not only did the various Christian communities win the
respect of their neighbours and so on occasion avoid the worst
elements of occasional persecution, but they also began to win
a religious and philosophical battle with the various pagan
alternatives of the day:

It [Christianity] offered certainty and won conviction where the
great venture of Greek philosophy was widely perceived to have
argued itself into the ground. By 250, it was still the persecuted
faith of a small minority, but its progress was sufficient to reflect
on a growing failure of the pagan towns.[5]

Prior to Constantine therefore we gain a picture of a church
that was beginning to address society both practically and
ideologically. The church acted out its scriptural understanding
of what that kingdom should look like and continued to
present the claims of the kingdom in both preaching and philosophical debate. It was on the basis of this growing success in
speaking to society that the church felt able to address also the
rulers of that society. That opportunity may have come without
a formal Christian ruler but the advent of such a ruler certainly
provided the occasion.[6]

The question of a formal relationship between the church as
an institution and the state did not arise before Constantine,
but the growing numerical strength of the church and the
rather obvious failure of persecution meant that the church
could not be ignored. Surprisingly, there had been earlier occa-
sions when the church had appealed to pagan emperors to
settle disputes between factious groups of Christians, although
these had been few and far between.

But once a Christian emperor had ascended to the throne, it

is easy to see how the expectations of the church rose markedly. Two prior events helped to sharpen those expectations. The ferocity of the Diocletian persecution was still well remembered. That final persecution had begun in 303 and had continued in the eastern part of the empire following the death of Diocletian in 305, until the year 311.

The generosity of Constantine in restoring property and land to those who had been persecuted even prior to his conversion sent out promising signals.[7] If a pagan emperor could be so generous, what might a Christian one do? Christians did not have to wait long to find out. Following Constantine's decisive military victory in 312, there came the Edict of Milan which offered official state toleration to Christians. Immediately following that edict, the influence of Constantine was felt in a number of ways.

First, the emperor was invited to intervene in various disputes, notably the schism between Donatists and Catholics in north Africa – a dispute that had been caused largely because of tensions over the issue of "the lapsed", and particularly over a bishop who had handed over the scriptures of the church to be burnt. That initial intervention in church matters continued and was felt very clearly in the various councils of the church, beginning with the council at Arles and crucially at the council of Nicaea in 325.

Second, Constantine ensured that significant financial patronage allowed prestigious church building projects to take place in many cities in the empire. This state patronage, previously enjoyed by pagan cults, paved the way for the third area of influence. In 325 Constantine's policy changed from that of mere toleration and sponsorship of Christianity to make Christianity the official religion of the empire.

Such a development was not so remarkable in that various emperors had given particular prominence to their own favoured pagan cult. It might even have been expected that Constantine would do the same for his religious community.

The difference lay in the perceived departure from the promotion of one god chosen from a pagan panoply of gods to that of a single Christian God. That was a new development for the empire. The official status given to Christianity did not mean that paganism was no longer tolerated. Indeed, Constantine insisted that pagans should live alongside Christians and should be convinced by debate and not by other inducements.

The fourth development in Constantine's period was that he wrote letters on behalf of the Christian faith publicly advocating the cause of Christianity. That public identification had its impact. Towns who petitioned the emperor cited their Christian faith as a reason for his patronage at the same time as drawing his attention to the other amenities and benefits of the town.[8]

The fifth action of Constantine was to use the church as a means of distributing food and welfare. There is no evidence that the church abused its use of such resources to coerce conversion but the very fact that the church was seen as a conduit of considerable charity helped its public image. The combination of the changed legal status of Christianity, its financial patronage such that impressive and very public churches (sermons in stone) could be built, the advocacy of the truth of the Christian faith by the emperor and the increasing number of laws that favoured the Christian community, changed the position of the church dramatically.

The quality of converts that arose from the growing social status of the faith was not always high. Some saw the social and financial advantage that could flow from conversion. Even during Constantine's reign we see local churches issuing rulings concerning those Christians who entered pagan temples and sacrificed to pagan gods after their baptism. There are even accounts of individuals pretending to be Christian clerics in order to claim the financial benefit of exemption from the expense of fulfilling civic duties.[9]

THE MEANING OF MISSION

It is possible to argue that the vast improvement in the social standing of the church highlighted a subtle shift that had been gradually taking place in the first few centuries of the life of the Christian community. At first, the church thought only of mission. Spurred on by the thought of the imminent return of the Lord (the eschaton) there was an urgency to focus on the spread of the faith rather than thinking about the shape of the church.

In other words the Christian community engaged in mission and the church was shaped by mission. The absence of the eschaton gradually allowed Christians to think more about the church and its doctrines. The arrival of social status meant that mission was now something that the church performed as one of its many functions and not its sole activity. In that sense, mission was becoming the preserve of the institution rather than the people of God, of the professionals rather than those who sat in the pew. The nature of the church began to shape the mission of the church rather than mission giving shape to the church – a subtle but crucial change.

That change in the meaning and function of mission began to be seen more acutely shortly after the death of Constantine. Constantine was more tolerant of his pagan subjects than those who followed and it was not long before there came a growing demand for increasing degrees of pressure to be placed on people to become Christians when mere advocacy failed. As early as 340 we can find writings which advocate the banning of pagan worship and the destruction of pagan temples. Constantius II (337–361) and Theodosius I (379–395) gradually forbad public sacrifices and closed temples. On occasion, there were some spectacular acts of destruction, for example, that of the gigantic Serapeum of Alexandria in 391. But these were not initiatives of the civil authority so much as the popular will of the people with which the authorities colluded.[10]

The complexity of these kinds of interactions can be seen in the ministry of Martin of Tours who became bishop of that city in 372. Martin's ministry had been inspired by the desert fathers and he attracted a considerable following of those who wished to live a monastic life. Martin is credited with founding monasticism in the West. As with most of the major towns in the Western empire, the city of Tours was largely Christian by the time of Martin's appointment. But the surrounding countryside was still decidedly pagan. That was a state of affairs that Martin was determined to rectify.

He engaged in his mission with a variety of approaches. In part he preached and attempted to win converts. To some extent he caught the attention of the people simply because he was a holy man and a rather dynamic one at that. But he also engaged in tactics of considerable confrontation. On one occasion, Martin is credited with attempting to chop down a tree that was venerated by local pagans. Needless to say, his desire provoked a furious response. The pagan leaders made a suggestion to Martin. They would chop down the tree if he would stand at the spot where they thought the tree would fall. Martin accepted the challenge and the contest began. The story continues:

> Accordingly since that pine tree was hanging over in one direction so that there was no doubt to what side it would fall on being cut, Martin, having been bound, is, in accordance with the decision of these pagans, placed in that spot where, as no one doubted, the tree was about to fall. They began therefore to cut down their own tree, with great glee and joyfulness, while there was at some distance a great multitude of wondering spectators.[11]

The story contains dramatic and familiar themes. Martin's followers were anxious, but he was confident and put his trust in God. Most important of all, when the deliverance from danger took place, pagan and Christian alike believed a miracle had occurred. Then, numerous conversions took place, "For there was hardly one of that immense multitude of heathens who did not express a desire for the imposition of hands, and abandoning his impious errors, made a profession of faith in Jesus."[12]

There is no doubt that on occasion, Martin and his followers did destroy local pagan temples but it is difficult to suggest that the local populace was deeply disturbed by these developments. Martin's reputation as a holy man went before him. It is true that he was protected to a degree by the authorities of the time which gave official sanction to Christianity but that would hardly have protected him from a furious local mob.

The clue to this complex transaction probably lies in the very use of the word "pagan". It was a word that originally meant "second-class participant" and it could be used by regular soldiers to describe mere civilians or by high officials to describe lower officials. Over time the term came to be applied to country dwellers, presumably because they had less status than townsfolk.[13] Those who were polytheists gradually became referred to as those who had the religion of these lesser country folk. They were therefore pagans. The alternative word is that of "heathen" – those who lived on the heath or countryside.

The point is that Christianity now had standing in the community. Those who had formally opposed them to the point of persecution were now merely second class citizens – pagans or heathens. Christianity was in the ascendancy and that was partly a matter of power and prestige but only rarely a matter of persecution. That bold statement carries with it some exceptions. (Notably, and to the shame of the church, Jews were persecuted from an early time.)

THE COMPLEXITY OF CHRISTENDOM

Many authors suggest that Christendom as a functioning

reality existed from the time of Constantine's Edict of Milan in 313 until the First Amendment of the US Constitution in 1791.[14] The reason for the choice of this latter date relates to the conscious separation of church and state. But there are many reasons to suppose that the underlying reality of Christendom continued much beyond this date until at least the 1950s. A formal separation of function did not mean that those who ran the secular institutions of the West did not have a deep commitment to a Christian worldview even when they were not conscious of so doing. It is certainly arguable that the leaders of Christian churches in the West assumed until the late 1950s that the moral framework provided by Christianity operated as the moral framework for the secular state. That helps to explain the sense of shock in the 1960s when that assumption began to be challenged.

But whatever date one chooses for the endpoint of a Christendom framework, it is clear that Christendom in the West has existed for the greatest part of the life of the church and to live without such a familiar set of assumptions brings a degree of demoralisation and confusion to the church. It is also clear that Christendom has existed in a number of forms and is therefore a complex reality. That is important because if we are to see Christendom as a primary cause and culprit in replacing a concern for mission with a tendency for the church to promote its own life as an end in itself, then we have to see that the charge is not always accurate. There are at least four distinct forms of Christendom that we need to be aware of.

1. Christendom in the Eastern Empire

Those of us who live in the West are inclined to forget that the empire continued long after the fall of Rome in the form of the Byzantine Empire. Although the formal break between the churches of the East (the Orthodox churches) and the church of the West (the Catholic church) did not take place until 1054, the separate development of East and West meant that there was a considerable difference in the ethos and interests of these churches. The Eastern church was identified with the empire to such an extent that it was sometimes difficult to separate the interests of the two. Persian Christians were viewed with suspicion and sometimes persecuted precisely because Christianity was so identified with the empire and the Persians were often in conflict with that same empire.

It is sometimes claimed that the dominant theme of mission in the Eastern church springs from their undoubted love for the gospel of John. Mission is not so much designed to win individual conversion, though that is still present, but has a profound concern for the restoration and sanctification of the whole universe. There is a cosmic dimension to mission which includes society, the state, culture and nature.[15] All are to be redeemed and restored to their true calling as reflecting the image of God who brought them into being in the first place.

In this regard the liturgy becomes central as an acting out of the drama of cosmic salvation. For the Orthodox, mission is the "liturgy after the liturgy". The action of demonstrating God's love for the world which comes after the liturgy has ended, is also worship. Orthodox Christians engaged in mission by spreading the faith to the lands that lay to the north of the empire – into much of Eastern Europe and to Russia. Their concern within the empire was often the intellectual challenge that arose from combating many heresies. For the Orthodox that too is mission. The strong identification of the church with mission means that mission can become synonymous with the expansion of the church, its liturgy and its influence in society. In situations where the church has been in a minority position, for example when operating in majority Muslim countries, there can come a tendency to become introverted and concerned for the survival of the church almost as an end in itself.

2. The Early Medieval Period

After the year 400 the Western empire was under increasing pressure from Germanic tribes that were invading from the north and the east. The first serious incursion into the territory of the empire came in 404 when Gaul was invaded. In the years that followed, Rome was sacked twice until the Western empire ceased in any recognisable form in 476. The missionary task of the church now changed dramatically. The task of winning over the population of the empire had largely been completed by the year 400. Now the task of bringing the faith to these new populations of invaders began.

The task was not a simple matter and was probably not complete until more than 600 years after the invasions began when the northernmost reaches of Europe finally came to faith. The decisive period was that of the first 200 years when early medieval Europe gradually emerged from what the historians often call "the dark ages" – the period when the light of learning went out.

Two remarkable and very different parallel missionary movements played a huge part in the reconversion of Western Europe. Both were monastic in inspiration but were substantially different in their theology, practice and understanding of mission and the church. One movement is associated with the Celtic saints and in recent years their place in the reconversion of Europe has been given much more prominence. Interestingly, their major impetus came from outside of the boundaries of the old empire.

Irish monks and nuns, emerging from a society only recently converted from a pagan past, made a huge impact on the new tribes that had entered Europe. Following the river valleys of Europe, the wandering Celts established Christian communities from Scotland to Italy and from Spain to Austria. Although they certainly preached to kings and rulers, their primary target was that of ordinary people. Their passion for mission profoundly shaped the churches that they planted.

While the Celts expanded as a vast missionary enterprise, the Roman church also used monks of a rather different kind to establish the church in large parts of Europe. Their mission often focussed on a mission to the new rulers of Europe and at the very least the patronage of the nobility was sought in order to establish their mission work. In this, they could rely on the undoubted prestige that the Roman church began to enjoy. They were able to convey a sense that to be civilised, to be a true new European, it was necessary to become Christian.

Their mission goal was to establish the church and to welcome people into the church. And it was the church that they brought. They did not just bring missionaries but fully formed church structures which often included a bishop. Unlike the Celts for whom the bishop was subject to the missionary community, Roman bishops were clearly in charge of the missionary enterprise. Their desire was to establish a diocese. The formation of a fully formed church structure was inseparable from the missionary enterprise. The early Celtic missions, by contrast, left very little in the form of institutions and buildings. Instead they engaged in mission and the church was what mission created.

It is sometimes suggested that while the Celts broke fresh ground, the Romans followed up and organised that which the Celts had pioneered. That is a little over simplified as a statement but nevertheless carries a great deal of truth in terms of an overall theme.

3. The Later Medieval Period

The missionary work of both the Celts and the Romans produced a largely Christian Europe. It is difficult to produce an exact date for the later medieval period. Some would date it from Pope Gregory the Great (590–604) and although this is perhaps a little early, the themes of a later, post-Charlemagne

(771–814) Europe can be traced back to this period. The earlier thinking of Augustine to the effect that there was no salvation outside of the church eventually became the basis of a society in which the role of church and state were well defined. In that definition, state and church were connected in a single civilisation and worldview. In such a situation state and church needed each other. In that kind of world, it was unthinkable that the subjects of a Christian king would not also be Christians. As one writer puts it:

> Thus the enforced baptism of the Saxons was a natural consequence of their defeat at the hands of Charlemagne. They had to be baptized, even against their will if they refused, *because* they had been conquered. Subjection to the stronger God followed subjection to the victorious ruler as a matter of course. Once baptized, the Saxons faced execution if they reverted to their traditional faith; it was inconceivable that they could be politically loyal if their religious loyalty was doubted. The same pattern would repeat itself elsewhere: Olav Tryggvason's violent Christianization of Norway in the late tenth century, the subjugation, in the twelfth century of the Wends who lived east and north of the Elbe, and so forth.[16]

Such a view of mission was never practised by the earlier Celtic missions but in the later medieval West, the expansion of the church and its integration with a total worldview was synonymous. " . . . the structure of human society was finally and permanently ordered and nobody was to tamper with it."[17]

In such a system, the mission of the church became the attempt to thoroughly Christianise society and even on occasion to renew the church in its spiritual purity and its doctrinal understanding. Mission was what the church did as an expression of its life within Christendom. There was virtually no attempt to engage in mission outside of the boundaries of Christendom.

4. The Post-Reformation Period

The medieval period had witnessed a number of renewal movements which were aimed at purifying the church. These were almost always focussed around monastic movements and often gave rise to new monastic orders. In the view of many historians, the Reformation made possible the foundations of the modern world but strictly speaking it began as yet another medieval reforming movement. It is not a coincidence that the first catalyst of the Reformation, Martin Luther, was himself a monk.

The aims of the Reformers were not so very different from those of the leaders of earlier medieval renewal movements. In common with the outlook of the medieval world, they believed that church and state should work in a complete partnership to produce a Christian society. But the consequences of the Reformation were not exactly what the founders expected. The division of the church led to a series of religious wars in Europe which produced a very different relationship between church and state to that which had prevailed previously. Power shifted from church to state with the state becoming the sole arbiter of religious settlements. Some thinkers believe that the origins of the modern secular state begin with the Reformation and not solely with the later Enlightenment period of the 18th century.

The Reformation's emphasis on the individual's relationship with God and on the priesthood of all believers introduced ideas that could not be contained within an entirely medieval worldview. One minority view that developed early on in the Reformation period was that of the Anabaptists. From their perspective the relationship between church and state needed to be broken. Their desire was to return to a simpler pre-Constantian view of the church, that of a brotherhood that reflected the New Testament picture of a church set apart from the world. From their perspective the whole of Europe was in

fact a mission field. The Anabaptists experienced severe persecution such that many left Europe for the new world of the
Americas.

Their ideas were picked up somewhat later by the 18th
century Pietists. They were not as radical in their vision of the
ideal Christian community, but they did emphasise the importance of the individual's relationship with God. The notion of
a crisis experience of conversion was adopted by Wesley and
the evangelical revivalists. The revivalists did not exactly think
of Europe as a mission field, though Wesley's notion of the
whole world as his parish came close. Wesley and his compan-
ions never imagined that they had not been Christians before
their crisis experience of "the heart strangely warmed" but they
did believe that this was a vital key to unlocking true holiness.
They began to promote the idea of conversion as a revival of
true faith, the product of evangelism. For evangelicals there
came a separation in their thinking between evangelism which
was to be conducted in the hinterlands of Christian Europe
and North America and mission which was to be conducted
outside of Christendom.

The experience of the crisis of conversion was given very
definite methodological structure, in particular by North
American revivalists such as Charles Finney. Moody, in the
late 19th century, Billy Sunday in the early 20th century and
Billy Graham in the middle to late 20th century, continued that
tradition. The evangelical tradition developed an approach to
the Christian faith which strongly identified evangelistic methods as an approach which could strengthen the church in
Christendom. Taking the church to other lands was seen as the
purpose of mission.

Once again, though in a different framework, mission was
seen as a means of growing the church overseas and evangelism
as a means of strengthening the church at home. But no matter
whether at home or overseas the expansion of the church
tended to become the chief end of both evangelism and

mission. Mission was something that the church did to prosper its own life and witness. Evangelicals did have a vision of a changed society but that tended to be an outcome of a strengthened church and not a part of mission as such. For evangelicals evangelism and mission were essentially programmes of the church, something that faithful churches did.

Today we stand on the other side of Christendom. Some explicitly refer to the West as post-Christian. No one seriously argues that Christendom in any substantial form still exists. The notion of the secular has come to mean that which is opposed to religion. In such a situation, the church has been forced to look afresh at its context, to consider the post-Christian West as a mission field. The church in the West has been assisted by the arrival of missionaries from those very lands that were the original target of the modern missionary movement. But to think of our context as a mission field is a very long way from becoming a missionary church.

The challenge for the church now is to stop thinking merely about methods to reverse decline but to reconsider the basic purpose and call of the church. To return to mission as the core *raison d'être* of the church will inevitably mean that the shape of the church will change. Our very failure may well assist us to return to that innovation stage of the life of the church when the church ceases to do church but to do mission. What flows from mission will still be the church but it will be a very different kind of church. We now have to begin to consider what that mission might look like so that we can prepare the church for mission.

NOTES

1. Hans Küng, *On Being a Christian*, Collins, 1997, p. 285.
2. Alister E McGrath, *Christian Theology: An Introduction*, 1994, p. 405.

3. Küng, *On Being a Christian*, p. 478.
4. Robin Lane Fox, *Pagans and Christians in the Mediterranean World from the Second Century A.D. to the Conversion of Constantine*, Penguin, 1986, p. 335.
5. Ibid.
6. Oliver O'Donovan, *The Desire of the Nations: Rediscovering the Roots of Political Theology*, Cambridge University Press, 1996, p. 193.
7. Lane Fox, *Pagans and Christians in the Mediterranean World*, p. 611.
8. Ibid., p. 638.
9. Ibid., p. 668.
10. Peter Brown, *The Rise of Western Christendom*, Blackwell, 1996, p. 35.
11. Christopher Donaldson, *Martin of Tours: The Shaping of Celtic Spirituality*, Routledge, 1980, p. 110.
12. Ibid., p. 111.
13. Brown, *The Rise of Western Christendom*, p. 35.
14. O'Donovan, *The Desire of the Nations*, p. 195.
15. David Bosch, *Transforming Mission*, Orbis, 1991, p. 209.
16. Ibid., p. 224.
17. Ibid., p. 225.

CHAPTER THREE

CHANGING THE INTERACTION

Faced with the problem of the decline of the church, the understandable reaction of those who are concerned to bring change is to concentrate on what it would take to make the church effective in its mission. In one sense that it also what this book is about. But there is a subtlety here which must not be missed. Social institutions, such as the church, do not exist in isolation from their context. What is at stake here is much more than beefing up the programmes of the church so that congregations can attract more members. The challenge is not just to make the church effective in its own life and witness but to do so in such a way that the core interaction with the culture is changed.

What does such a change really mean? If you were to be asked the question, "Does the church significantly influence our culture or is it the culture that significantly influences the church?", what would your reply be? Almost certainly you would be likely to suggest that over the last few decades, the culture has influenced the church much more than the church has influenced the culture. That is not so everywhere. Ask the same question of church leaders in Ghana and you will receive the answer that the church influences the culture more than the other way round. If the church was operating in such a way that the culture was significantly influenced by it, not only would something have happened to the church itself but its relationship with the broader society would clearly be different from what it is at the moment. In short, the basic interaction between church and culture would have changed.

Whenever church leaders consider the findings of Loren Mead,[1] they recognise immediately the truth of the notion that the single biggest factor in determining whether or not people come to church resides in what they think of the church. In short, those who live in our community are significantly influenced by whether or not the church has a social value. I am not suggesting that people only join churches when they see a social advantage in doing so, though such motives have been ascribed to churchgoers on occasion. But clearly it is much more likely that people will respond favourably to the witness of the church when the church is well regarded. The way in which we live and bear witness significantly influences the view that the wider community has of the church.

The reality that I am pointing to has a long heritage. We read in Acts of the Apostles that the church grew as a direct consequence of the fact that the apostles enjoyed the favour of all the people (Acts 5:12–14).

That basic principle, namely that the church needs to be well regarded by the surrounding community in order to grow, seems like a very mundane observation but it is surprising how often the point is missed. Why should this be? Perhaps in part it is because there is often a linkage with events that indicate the dramatic intervention of God. So, for example, in Acts 5 the growth of the favour of the people flows directly in the passage from the fact that the apostles worked many signs and wonders. Is it then always essential for the miraculous to be present in order for the Christian community to be well regarded by the wider community or can other factors be just as important?

The scholar Alan Kreider has conducted a valuable study into the factors that led individuals to become Christians in the centuries prior to the foundation of Christendom at the time of Constantine. Kreider's account of how conversion took place is fascinating precisely because Christians were not officially well regarded and there was certainly no social advantage in becoming a Christian. Indeed in times of persecution the exact reverse was the case.

The heart of Kreider's case is that Christians came to be well regarded by those who had a personal acquaintance either with Christian communities or with individual Christians through a curious combination of factors. There was certainly the miraculous, seen in healings and exorcisms. There was also their ability to cross social divides and to create an authentic community in which the poor and women could hold positions of honour in relation to the gifting and calling of God, rather than to social standing. In addition there was the astonishing practice of generous and spontaneous goodness especially to the poor and needy.

Kreider offers the following story as an illustration of that latter point:

A fascinating example comes from early fourth-century Egypt, where press gangs were abducting peasants and shipping them down the Nile for service in the Roman legions. In Thebes the Christian church heard of conscripts in their local jail; the military authorities had put them there to prevent them from escaping before they transported them further. When the Christians heard that the prisoners were in distress, they brought them food, drink and other necessities. One of the conscripts, Pachomius, asked what was going on. The people coming to his aid, he was told, were Christians who "are merciful to everyone, including strangers". Pachomius had never heard of Christians, so he asked for more information.

"They are people who bear the name of Christ, the only begotten Son of God, and they do good to everyone, putting their hope in

Him who made the heaven and earth and us humans." (First Greek Life of Pachomius 4–5)

Inspired by the Christians' visit and material aid, Pachomius sought as much solitude as was possible in the prison, where he offered to God a prayer of conditional commitment: "If you will deliver me from this affliction, I will serve your will all the days of my life." Shortly thereafter, Pachomius – who was to become the prime mover of early conventual monasticism – was discharged, whereupon he went to a church where he was instructed and baptized.[2]

This core case, namely that it was the attractive behaviour of Christians that attracted many to the faith can be made from many other periods of the Christian church. Take for example the mission of the Celtic saints in many parts of Europe. While it is certainly true that the Celtic missionaries were well known for the miracles associated with their ministries, they were just as well known for the compassion that they exercised towards the poor.

St Cuthbert, one of the best known figures in the early Celtic church in Northumbria, was renowned for his work amongst the poor. The church historian, Bede, offers a number of stories which highlight such a concern. He tells of how the king of Northumbria gave one of his best horses to Cuthbert because he was aware that his advancing years made it difficult for him to walk. It was not long before he discovered that the horse was gone and Cuthbert was walking again. It was not due to carelessness that the horse had departed. Rather, Cuthbert had sold the horse so that the proceeds could be given to the poor.

Cuthbert was famous for his frequent journeys to inaccessible areas of the kingdom for the sole purpose of preaching to the poor who might otherwise never have heard the Christian message. The integrity of such pioneers of the faith turned the hearts of the people to the message of Christ. They won the favour of the people, not just by virtue of their wonder-working miracles but more by their honest compassion. The witness of concern vividly demonstrated the authenticity of a message which spoke of the grace and love of God.

As Bishop Michael Nazir-Ali suggests:

Such a "turning" to God and dependence upon him bring about a metamorphosis or transformation of our inward being (Romans 12:2), so that our hearts overflow with love for God and for our neighbours. As Anna of *Mister God, This is Anna* saw very well, such transformation comes because God can "kiss you right inside".[3]

So, in our quest to reach the world with the gospel, is it sufficient merely to "let our light shine before men"? Is the witness of good works all that is needed in order to win the favour of men? Is this what is required in order to change what Mead calls the "basic interaction between religious institutions and the nature of our social environment"?

Inevitably the generation of a movement that transforms society is always a more complex matter than any single factor on its own, no matter how potent that factor might be. It is certainly possible to point to situations where patient Christian witness of exactly the kind that impacted Pachomius has produced very little result indeed.

However that is not to say that the exercise of changing the mind of a culture or a society about the value of the Christian church – changing the basic interaction between church and society – is not an important and essential ingredient in the creation of a transforming movement. It certainly is. But the way in which that change operates in relation to other factors is always complex.

One way to glimpse that complexity is to look afresh at the growth of the Christian movement following the revivals in Great Britain from the middle of the 18th century through to the middle of the 19th century. This particular example is all the more valuable precisely because the revivals associated with Wesley and Whitefield are often looked to as a model by many who desire to see the church grow in our time. In this model, signs and wonders, the miraculous dimension of Christian encounter is seen as primary. The emphasis from the Acts passage would certainly be on the wonderful deeds performed by the apostles more than the quiet witness that won Pachomius.

The cry goes up, "Please God, send a revival." The implication is that in the matter of the sending of revivals we are essentially helpless other than to pray more, to live holy lives, perhaps withdraw more from the world, search for an intensity of ecstatic experience, seek a blessing from God, look for a miracle, or search for anointed preachers.

Others have looked to the revivals of South America and heard the message that the revivals there were brought about by the unified prayers of leaders from different Christian traditions coming together to pray for revival. Taken to its logical conclusion, it is almost possible to argue that divine intervention in the form of revival is itself close to a methodological formula. United prayer and forgiveness within the Christian community produces an outpouring of the Holy Spirit in a revival that impacts the whole community.

That is certainly a model that many evangelicals find attractive. Like many, both in Britain and America, with an evangelical schooling, I have imbibed the idea that the revivals of the mid- to late 18th century saved both nations from huge social evil, and in the case of Britain from something akin to the French Revolution. Being caught up in a degree of romanticism with respect to those revivals, it is all too easy to wish that one could have been present at the time, to witness the profound changes in the lives of those impacted by the revival. Touring Britain, that sense of wonder concerning the revivals is constantly reinforced by the many plaques in towns across the land that proclaim, "John Wesley preached here."

It can be a source of surprise to read the accounts of Christians who were living some 40 or 50 years after the revivals began, at a time when Wesley was at the end of his ministry. Evangelicals tend to imagine that this was precisely the time when it would have been wonderful to be a Christian, to see the fruits of revival, to witness the impact on the nation. Unfortunately, that is not what we read. The contemporary accounts of Christian leaders at this time were almost universally pessimistic about the future of the nation. Moreover they seemed to think that the Christian impact on the nation was very limited and the churches still weak. That is not what most evangelical Christians imagine to be the case after more than 40 years of revival.

What then was the situation around the year 1800 and why were Christian leaders so pessimistic about the future prospects for church and nation? We do have to remember what had prevailed before the revivals broke out. The early 18th century witnessed a Britain with a small and secret Roman Catholic church, outlawed and underground, a defeated non-conformist community and a Church of England in serious need of reform.

The non-conformists had lost out in the settlement that followed the Restoration of the crown in 1660 and in any case had lost much moral authority because of the excesses of the Commonwealth period under Cromwell. Their reaction had frequently been to retreat into a kind of hyper-Calvinism that saw evangelism as both unnecessary and dangerous, lest the wrong people – those that God had not elected – tried to respond to salvation. Just prior to the revivals, it has been estimated that the total non-conformist community numbered no more than 2.5% of the population.

The Church of England, victorious as it was as a result of the Restoration settlement, suffered from the sins that flowed from its status as an established church. Multiple benefices were rife with clergy occupying a number of parishes and so being absent a good deal of the time. The education of the clergy was sadly lacking with many unable to preach a sermon. Even some of those well educated and present in their parish were sometimes eccentric to say the least. There was the famous case of a clergyman who believed that God could only be approached and understood properly in the Hebrew language. He was a good scholar and preached all of his sermons entirely in Hebrew, to the bemusement of his congregation. The ineffectiveness of the church in relation to their immediate communities was reflected in a lack of influence on national life.

The scholar Herbert Schlossberg records some of the decline experienced by the established church in the 18th century:

Bishop Butler of Hereford compared Church attendance in his diocese in 1792 with the numbers from 1747 and found a substantial decline. In 1800 in the diocese of Lincoln, England's largest, Evangelical clergymen found that of 15,000 persons in 79 parishes, fewer than 5,000 were known to attend Church; of these, only 1,800 were communicants. Many of the nonattenders had gone over to Dissent, but there was still a very low level of religious participation. In 1799, Bishop Cleaver of Chester, a highly industrial region, discovered a parish of 40,000 in which nobody attended religious services of any kind.[4]

The revivals associated with Wesley and Whitefield began in 1739, and continued in localised expressions for a generation. Why then did these revivals, so fondly regarded by later evangelicals, seen by many as a model to which the contemporary church should look, seem to Christian leaders at the end of the 18th century to have had such little impact? Two factors seem to be important.

First, the numbers involved in the revivals were not as great as we might popularly imagine. It is very difficult to discover precise figures, but the romanticised impression left with evangelicals that the revivals swept the country with the whole nation feeling the impact seems to be an exaggeration. Apart from anything else, it is instructive to read the diaries of Wesley and see how often he speaks of unreceptive towns and situations.

Can we know anything about the numbers impacted? Clearly it is hard to estimate how many evangelicals remained in the Church of England. Equally it is hard to know how many were touched by the revivals and remained as members of the various non-conformist churches. The only certain figures we have relate to those who were members of the various Methodist societies. Some figures from 1775, fully 35 years after the first outbreak of revival, give some information.

Particular Baptists	9,000
Congregational	22,000
Methodists	30,000

It is not too likely that many from the revival found their way into the Particular Baptists, although some may have joined the Congregational churches. We also need to remember that the criteria for membership was rigorous and there would have been some who were influenced by the revival and therefore not recorded in those figures. We also need to remember that the population of Britain was approximately one sixth of what it is today. However, even allowing for all these factors, the figure of 30,000 Methodists does not represent the kind of widespread growth that is sometimes imagined by evangelicals of a later generation.

While it certainly represents significant growth for a movement that had started from nothing 35 years earlier, is it really any more significant than the growth of the New Churches in Britain from the early 1970s until today which is put at about 200,000 people? More interesting still, it is very small when compared with the growth of Methodism during the next 35 to 40 years. One is bound to ask what caused the massive growth after the first flush of revival had ended, as compared with the relatively modest gains of the first 35 years. Is it the case, as some have argued, that a head of steam had built up and the massive growth of the next period was purely incremental expansion on the wave of earlier enthusiasm? Would anybody like to argue that the New Churches will expand by 500% in the next 40 years as a result of incremental growth? If not, why not?

The second factor is even more critical. Apart from the numbers being insufficient to make a dramatic impact on society simply by virtue of the weight of numbers, it is clear to most observers that the evangelicals, or enthusiasts, as they were sometimes called, stood at the margins of society. It was not just a matter of social class, though that must have played its part; it was also the case that they suffered from what we might call today a seriously bad press.

It doesn't require a great deal of exposure to Wesley's journals to discover that his normative experience consisted of many more hostile encounters than revival joy. Three illustrations give something of the flavour of those perspectives.

First, the historian Mary Heimann says this of the Methodists:

> Methodists, who harangued from the pulpit or met in open fields to proclaim the Gospel, like Jansenists, who writhed convulsively at the Saint-Medard cemetery, seemed to be wild, unpredictable folk, rabble-rousers and hysterics who, as often as not, were drawn from the most dangerous ranks of society – those who had least to lose by its overthrow. It is therefore not altogether surprising that the "religion of the mob" which they seemed to represent was generally attacked with satire rather than with reasoned debate and treated to loathing rather than to measured criticisms, even by those who prided themselves on their universality, toleration and advocacy of open debate.[5]

Second, it is abundantly clear that it was not just the religious mob that faced loathing. The evangelical message itself faced ridicule, particularly in the face of what we call today the "chattering classes". Paul Johnson makes the following observation:

> The first Evangelical in Parliament, Sir Richard Hill, was lovingly described by the Reverend Edward Sidney, his biographer, as a model of a Christian gentleman and an upright senator. Hill quoted the Bible to the Commons, to "prolonged roars of laughter".[6]

Third, the assessment of the state of the nation by those such as William Wilberforce was profoundly pessimistic. Writing in 1797 he commented:

> If the representations contained in the preceding chapters, of the state of Christianity among the bulk of professed Christians, be not very erroneous, they may well excite serious apprehension in the mind of every reader, when considered merely in a political view. And this apprehension would be increased, if there should appear reason to believe that, for some time past, Religion has been on the decline among us, and that it continues to decline at the present moment.[7]

These quotations, together with many other pages of assessment and comment, paint a picture of a church that was still in deep difficulty even after many years of revival activity. Some openly predicted that the church would not survive the 19th century and indeed the huge challenges produced by rapid urbanisation were only just getting underway at the close of the 18th century.

Evangelicals were excluded from national life, not by public policy or by legislation, but by social pressure. They were regarded as narrow-minded, bigoted, lacking in humour, devoid of imagination, incapable of understanding the real world, occupying a subculture which normal people would not wish to enter. Those who were enticed into their circle were regarded as having met with an unfortunate accident, and no respectable family would willingly allow their offspring to be influenced in this way. Clearly it would be difficult to impact society from such a position. Although few, if any, living at that time, would have thought of it in this way, the basic inter-action between the evangelical movement and society had to be changed. That is precisely what did happen and it is that phenomenon that we need to examine.

CHANGING THE NATURE OF THE INTERACTION

The critical factor in the transformation of the relationship between evangelicals and the wider society flowed from the work of a group of evangelicals in national life who later became known as the Clapham Sect. The most notable member of the Clapham Sect was William Wilberforce, a member of parliament for his constituency of Hull. Wilberforce was best known for the central campaign of his life, the campaign to abolish slavery. He, more than anyone else, came to be associated with this single cause. However, his concerns were far wider than this single issue, no matter how significant a place that particular cause assumed.

Wilberforce was said to have been involved in at least 69 different causes, either as central campaigner or as a patron in some capacity. Although the campaigns in which he was involved were diverse, they had a number of commonalities. In general they were dedicated to improving the lot of the poor and disadvantaged. They formed part of a comprehensive view of society that essentially flowed from a biblical vision of soci-ety. For this reason, it is not surprising that Wilberforce was a founding father of the British and Foreign Bible Society. There is a sense in which this was the central jewel in a single vision of a society that was deeply influenced by the Christian message. The biblical narrative offered an inspiring vision of justice and of the basis for sound human relationships.

Wilberforce understood that it was not just a matter of working for legislative change in particular areas. First of all, public sentiment had to be shifted. The core assumptions of society needed to be challenged.

The campaign against slavery acutely illustrated the need for such a shift. When Wilberforce first argued against such an evil, he was met with an all too familiar response. In effect, his opponents were saying to him, if your conscience doesn't allow you to be involved with the slave trade, that's fine, you don't have to be involved; but make no mistake, others will take the place of any who drop out. In other words, the market rules and you can't buck it.

The notion of the invisible hand of the market was a fashionable idea. After all, it had first been popularised by Adam Smith in his work *The Wealth of Nations* published in 1776. But there was another force at work which pushed thinking in such a direction. The pernicious influence of groups like the Hell Fire Club, to which so many of society's opinion formers belonged, tended to encourage a deep cynicism about public life. The idea that those in public life were only really concerned to line their own pockets had gained a huge currency in the years prior to Wilberforce's involvement in political life. To some extent this cynicism can be laid at the door of Robert Walpole, who succeeded over a period of 40 years in shaping modern politics through the creation of the Whig party. Under Walpole, the Whigs became the natural party of government and self-interest throughout the middle of the 18th century.

The impact of these forces of self-interest was such that Wilberforce suggested that there was a new hypocrisy in the land. That hypocrisy was such that men had to pretend to be more evil than they actually were in order to gain credence. What a situation!

Wilberforce saw that a deeper change was needed than the mere passage of legislation. There was a need to change the whole political climate in which politicians and society operated. He needed to campaign to make goodness fashionable. The change of climate, of political sentiment, would make it more possible to change legislation. Without a fundamental shift of political vision it was unlikely that any of his plans for reform would succeed. In modern terms he needed to redefine the notion of political correctness so that it could be informed by a truly Christian vision of society.

The judgement of Wilberforce's contemporaries certainly indicates a recognition that fundamental change was taking place in the attitudes of society, and that this change was having a huge impact on receptivity to the gospel. The leading evangelical, Charles Simeon, writing in 1820 to a friend, the Reverend Thomas Truebody, made this comment:

> The numbers of pious clergy (i.e. Evangelical Anglican clergy) are greatly on the increase; how it is I know not for I do not think that either myself, or any other minister in the church, is very successful in converting souls to Christ. In my mind I ascribe it,
>
> 1. To God's secret blessings on the nation, on account of the attempts which are made to honour him in Britain.
> 2. To the influence of the Bible Society, which has given a kind of currency to gospel truths.[8]

It is clear then that something significant changed in the early years of the 19th century that was sufficiently important to bring hundreds of thousands into the churches. It was not the revival as such. To borrow the phrase used by Loren Mead, it is as if the interaction between religious institutions and the nature of their social environment was somehow altered so that the surrounding culture changed its view of the value of the church. That fundamental shift in the attitude of society to the church laid the foundations for the astonishing growth of the church in 19th century Britain.[9]

The contrast between the success of the church in the 19th century and its profound failure in the 18th century was commented on by the 19th century British Prime Minister, Gladstone:

> Riding in a stagecoach, a traveler (sic) heard this fragment of a conversation: "Well, what is the Church of England?" "The Church of England," came the reply, "is a damn big building with an organ inside." That is the way William Gladstone remembered the conversation and the way he told it at innumerable dinner parties for the remainder of his life. And that is the way English people tended to regard their Establishment in the waning years of the eighteenth century and for some time afterwards, which is the point Gladstone was making.[10]

Another way of thinking about that fundamental shift is to claim that the church formed by the revivals began to think primarily in terms of mission. That mission was directed towards winning individuals to faith but it was also sufficiently consumed with a vision of the kingdom that the transformation of society was just as important. The preoccupation of the church with mission caused the church to be shaped around mission and so to become an effective means of transforming both individuals and society as a genuine people movement. No one engaged in a campaign to abolish slavery in order to boost church attendance, yet paradoxically, by engaging first and foremost in mission the fortunes of the church were transformed.

NOTES

1. The research of Loren Mead was discussed in chapter one of this book.

2. Alan Kreider, *The Change of Conversion and the Origin of Christendom*, Trinity Press, 1999, p. 19f.

3. Michael Nazir-Ali, *Citizens and Exiles: Christian Faith in a Plural World*, SPCK, 1998, p. 49.

4. Herbert Schlossberg, *The Silent Revolution and the Making of Victorian England*, Ohio State University Press, 2000, p. 25.

5. Mary Heimann writing in *A World History of Christianity* (Ed, Adrian Hastings), Cassell, 1999, p. 475.

6. Paul Johnson, *A History of Christianity*, Simon and Schuster, 1995, p. 370.

7. William Wilberforce, *A Practical View of Christianity* (Ed, Kevin Charles Belmonte), Hendricksons, 1996, p. 191.

8. W Carus, *Memoirs of the Life of Rev Charles Simeon MA*, London, 1847, p. 536.

9. The case made by Herbert Schlossberg in the book cited above is that the foundations of Victorian England and the Victorian church were laid in the period 1780 to 1820.

10. Schlossberg, *The Silent Revolution and the Making of Victorian England*, p. 26f.

CHAPTER FOUR

CHEATING HISTORY

The historical record suggests that it is not easy for organisations, including individual congregations and more particularly denominations, to renew themselves. For every denomination that did succeed in the renewal process in past generations, it is possible to find many organisations and movements that simply withered away. However, despite the general record, there are some examples that suggest it is possible to cheat history, but we do need to recognise that it is not the norm. Is it possible to understand what happens when history is cheated?

It is worth taking a look again at the revival movements of the late 18th century to examine what took place, because in terms of the renewal of the Baptists, the Congregationalists and the Anglicans, history was indeed cheated. It is possible to look at the effects of the revival and to describe them under five headings or "fruits" of revival.

The first fruit of revival could be described as the remarkable conversion of some individuals, some of whom displayed strange behaviours. Under the unction or disturbance of profound spiritual encounter, ordinary people did some rather strange things which caused the respectable to view them with suspicion. They were considered by many in the wider society to be unstable, religious fanatics. What were some of these strange behaviours like? We can gain some idea from eye-witness accounts of the Cane Ridge revival which helped to initiate the Second Great Awakening in the United States.

> The dancing exercise. This generally began with the jerks, and was peculiar to professors of religion. The subject, after jerking awhile, began to dance, and then the jerks would cease. Such dancing was indeed heavenly to the spectators; there was nothing in it like levity, nor calculated to excite levity in the beholders . . . Sometimes the motion was quick and sometimes slow. Thus they continued to move forward and backward in the same track or alley till nature seemed exhausted, and they would fall prostrate on the floor or earth, unless caught by those standing by . . . .
>
> . . . The barking exercise (as opposers contemptuously called it) was nothing but the jerks. A person affected with the jerks, especially in his head, would often make a grunt, or bark, if you please, from the suddenness of the jerk. This name of barking seems to have had its origin from an old Presbyterian preacher of East Tennessee. He had gone into the woods for private devotion, and was seized with the jerks. Standing near a sapling, he caught hold of it, to prevent his falling, and as his head jerked back, he uttered a grunt or kind of noise similar to a bark, his face being turned upwards. Some wag discovered him in this position and reported that he found him barking up a tree.
>
> The laughing exercise was frequent, confined solely to the religious. It was a loud, hearty laughter, but one *sue generic*; it excited laughter in none else. The subject appeared rapturously solemn, and his laughter excited solemnity in saints and sinners. It is truly indescribable.[1]

The second fruit of revival followed on rather directly from the first, and could be described as the creation of new denominations – in the case of Britain in the 18th and 19th century, mostly varieties of Methodism. It is not difficult to see why new denominations were created given the unusual manifestations (or enthusiasm) which accompanied the outbreak of revival.

The third fruit of revival, which took much longer, could be described as the gradual renewal of the historic denominations. It is clear that by the late 18th century and early 19th century, the leadership of the historic churches was increasingly drawn from the evangelicals. The work of Charles Simeon illustrates this process in the Church of England, but parallels can be found amongst the other denominations also. Simeon was widely regarded as one of the key Anglican clerics whose ministry in Cambridge enabled many other evangelicals to remain in the Church of England. Not the least of his activities centred in the establishment of a Trust which bought the freeholds of many livings which then enabled evangelical clergy to be appointed. Herbert Schlossberg describes the work of Charles Simeon in some detail.[2]

The fourth fruit of revival was represented by the remarkable piece of social engagement pioneered by Wilberforce and the Clapham Sect but which actually went wider than that particular group. We looked at the activities of the Clapham Sect in the previous chapter. It was this revival fruit that produced a decisive change in the view of the wider population concerning the importance and value of the Christian church and of Christian commitment.

Arguably there is a fifth fruit to the revival which finds expression in the birth of the modern missionary movement. The present growth of the church around the world owes much to the creation of the modern missionary movement. Today, large numbers of Christians from the newer churches in South America, Africa and Asia are to be found in many Western nations. Some come very consciously as missionaries with the intention of re-evangelising the West. Others minister almost entirely amongst the ethnic groups from those continents who now live in the West on a semi-permanent basis. Some of the largest congregations in cities as diverse as Los Angeles,

Melbourne, London and Paris are composed largely of Christians from Africa, South America and Asia.

These phases of the revival stand in dynamic relationship to each other. For example, the historic churches would not have been renewed without the catalyst of the new denominations. A wider societal impact would not have taken place without the renewal of the historic churches. It is evident that the older denominations needed the enthusiastic involvement of Christians that had been influenced by the revival. It is also the case that no matter how vigorous the new denominations might be, they were not in a position to change the wider society without the sheer size and social influence that the historic denominations could offer. The growth of both newer and older denominations would not have taken place on the scale that it did without the social engagement that flowed from the reforming zeal of Wilberforce and his friends.

If this is an accurate read of that revival, might it not be possible to revisit what is happening today? Depending on what actually transpires in the next 20 years, two readings of our present situation would be possible.

Imagine that you were reading the comments of a social historian in the middle of the 21st century. One reading might be a comment on the final death of Christianity with one footnote. That detail would document that Christians thought that they had found a solution to their demise when the Charismatic Movement and the New Churches emerged on the scene. But this turned out to be a last gasp rather than a fresh breath.

The second alternative reading would be to note the astonishing growth of the church and its new place in society. Such a history would document that this all began with a revival movement in the middle 1960s that some called the Charismatic Movement. It produced strange phenomena including speaking in tongues. The second fruit was the creation of new denominations, first called the House

Churches and then (rather unimaginatively) the New Churches. Those new denominations grew vigorously but were unable by themselves to influence society as a whole.

The third fruit of revival was the gradual renewal of the historic churches as more and more members and more and more leaders were drawn from the ranks of evangelicals. That process caused them to think about mission and their relationship to their communities. As part of that process they began to think imaginatively about the nature and shape of the church. They began to work together in new cooperative ventures, building a passionate and vital commitment to the need to impact the world, not just with evangelistic endeavour but also with transformational action.

The fourth, and decisive, development was a remarkable piece of social engagement which took place amongst evangelicals in the first decade of the 21st century and which began to change the mood of the public about the value of the church and the place of virtue in public life. That was the key that helped to persuade the many to follow the way pioneered earlier by the few. If such a development did take place then it still might be possible for the church in the West today to cheat history.

But if that is what could happen, it is time to make a sober assessment of the situation of the church in the West at the beginning of the 21st century. There is good evidence to suggest that there are some signs of spiritual vigour in the overall life of the Christian community. There have been indications over the past 30 years of what we might call signs of revival. New denominations have emerged which have represented both an encouragement and a challenge to the historic denominations.

However, so far, there is little to indicate the significant renewal of the historic denominations. The careful observer might be able to point to some signs of hope but it would be fair to say that the future of the historic churches still hangs in the balance even though the influence of evangelicals in the ranks of most the historic denominations in the West has grown significantly in recent years. Given the importance of the potential renewal of the historic denominations to the over-all evangelisation of the West, we are bound to ask the question: what would it take to produce such a revitalisation? How can the church get from where it is to where it needs to be? Three elements would seem to be critical.

1. Church Planting

Church planting has not always enjoyed a good press. Unlike many nations in Africa, Asia and South America, where church planting is usually viewed as the normal sign of a healthy Christian community, existing congregations in the West have a tendency to see new church planting as a diversion of scarce resources from the revitalisation that they seek. The evidence of the benefit of church planting suggests that this is a mistaken perspective. Case histories of the few denominations in the West that have succeeded in revitalising the denomination through church planting suggest that new church plants grow faster and contribute more resources to the denomination than the resources they initially use. That tendency can be illustrated not only in the Western world but even in the younger mission fields that have appeared to be resistant to growth. One example would be that of Baptist churches in Bangladesh which have seen significant growth in recent years through investment in church planting.

Despite this knowledge, there seems to be a resistance on the part of many existing denominations to invest significantly in church planting. Of the larger historic churches in the United Kingdom, all engage in some peripheral church planting, that is to say less than 1% of their total number of congregations as church plants in a single year. To date none of the historic denominations have invested in the kind of dynamic movement-based church planting that would lead to a significant renewal of the denomination as a whole. We might describe that kind of church planting as transformative planting. To engage in that kind of activity, it would be necessary to envisage church planting on a scale of at least 3% of the total number of congregations in each year for at least ten years. Church planting on that scale leverages both growth and change. In short, it generates movement.

Why is that so? Primarily because sustaining church planting on such a scale requires significant change to take place in the sponsoring denomination. One case history that illustrates the point would be that of the Assemblies of God in Great Britain. The Assemblies represent a fascinating example because they fall somewhere between the model of historic denomination and new church.

Following the Dawn Congress held in Birmingham in 1992, the 630 Assemblies of God committed themselves to planting a further 1,000 congregations within ten years. That level of planting certainly qualifies as a transformative planting model. During the first few years, a significant amount of planting took place, certainly enough to be on target for their ten-year goal. A total of approximately 200 plants took place in the first three years but then, after that first flurry of activity, the planting stopped just as suddenly as it had begun. Not only did the planting stop but many of the plants that had already started did not succeed.

What had gone wrong? In reviewing their activity, the Assemblies recognised that several issues emerged. The first was that the initial plants represented the most obvious opportunities, and once the obvious had been exhausted there was no plan in place to locate the next wave of potential plants. Second, little attention had been paid to what had been planted so that one could argue that instead of 630 congregations, many of which were small and had problems, there were now a further 200 problems for the denomination to worry about. It could be argued that a model of church that needed change had now been replicated a further 200 times. Third, it was clear that in order to think differently about the kind of churches that were being planted and in order to have sufficient leaders to pioneer such work, a great deal needed to change in the denomination as a whole.

Embarking on a programme of transformative church planting demanded transformation in the denomination as a whole. Changing one significant area in a system carried the implication of changing everything. To their credit, the Assemblies of God have not abandoned church planting. Instead, they are facing the challenge of transforming the denomination, not least of all in terms of the training systems that are used. They are committed to the refocusing of their existing congregation towards mission, and have engaged around 100 congregations in a programme of mission discovery entitled "Journey into Mission". They recognise that this requires a commitment for the long haul.

Given that experience, it is perhaps not surprising that other denominations intuitively hold back from a commitment to church planting on such a scale. But in so doing they are almost certainly ignoring a key lever for renewal. Some, for example in the Church of England, argue that it is not feasible for a denomination of that size to engage in that scale of church planting. Certainly the sheer scale of the statistics look daunting. If one took the base figure of 17,000 existing parishes as the starting point for calculating the number of church plants that would be required to engineer change, that would produce 5,100 new parishes over a ten-year period.

Is there really room for that number of new Anglican parishes? Possibly not. But that argument misses a fundamental point about transformative planting. The skills required to church plant successfully can be utilised just as effectively in the renewal of congregations which are in difficulty. The situation of many parishes and congregations in the historic churches require that they be approached as replant situations. In many cases, nothing less radical will make the difference.

One example of just such a situation can be found in an inner-city United Reformed Church (URC). The church in question had struggled for many years. Temporary respite came through a merger with another URC congregation that had been located not more than a mile away. But it was not long before the same problems of decline and defeat reasserted themselves. Following a detailed examination of the problem, the URC District that had oversight of the situation closed the church and then reopened it a few moments later as a church plant.

Why such a strange approach? Mainly because this was the only way in which the District could introduce not only a new leadership but a new vision of what the church needed to be in that situation. As a church plant, a new congregation came to thrive in exactly the same building and locality in which the earlier congregation (earlier by a few minutes) had failed. Church planting skills can help in renewal just as much as they are required to launch successful new plants. Are there 5,100 parishes in the Church of England that would benefit from renewal? I am not aware that such research has been undertaken, but it is entirely possible that there are!

2. Intentional Leadership Development

Whenever a new church plant or a replant begins to take its mission context seriously, then inevitably the focus on mission begins to reshape the church. In other words, missional purpose impacts the nature and shape of the church. It doesn't take much imagination to realise that a missionally driven church requires a missional leadership to allow it to function in a healthy manner. What then is missional leadership? The most basic definition of missional leadership is drawn from the description of ministry gifts in Ephesians chapter four.

There we read that some were given grace or gifts to enable

them to be apostles, some prophets, some evangelists, some pastors and some teachers. The insight that these ministry descriptors might be important for the renewal of the church is not new. It re-emerged in the 19th century amongst the Irvingites and in the early 20th century amongst the various "apostolic" strands of the Pentecostal movement. More recently, the Charismatic Movement began to emphasise these leadership gifts from the 1970s onwards. However, much of the rest of the church has tended to view such an emphasis with suspicion. In part this is because the Irvingites, the Pentecostal apostolics and some of the newer Charismatic denominations tended to view these gifts as "offices" which were synonymous with authority. The track record of this approach has not always been very happy.

However, it is not necessary to equate such gifts with offices and as long ago as the mid-1970s some writers and theologians in the Charismatic Movement[3] were arguing that these gifts should be seen as core leadership qualities rather than actual offices. Their view was that the church, in the context of Christendom, had over-identified ministry with the gifts of pastor and teacher and had tended to ignore the other gifts as necessary only in the initial birthing of the church.

It does not take much imagination to see how that tendency developed. Clearly, in a situation when the whole population could be expected to be either actually or nominally Christian, it is clear that the major task of ministry is to help Christians understand their faith better (the teaching gift) or to care for the Christian community (the pastoral gift). The other gifts therefore tend to be under-utilised to the point where they are not identified with the normal ministry of the church. Once that position has been normalised it tends to become a self-reinforcing cycle. Ministers are identified as people with pastoral and teaching gifts. The recruitment processes of denominations become orientated towards the selection of people with those gift mixes.

Training systems are designed to help people become better pastors and teachers. Has any theological or Bible college developed training to help people become better apostles, prophets and evangelists?[4]

The product of such training further shapes the thinking of the church as to what ministry looks like and so the next cycle of recruitment is further orientated in such a direction until it eventually becomes impossible for those with apostolic, prophetic and evangelistic gifts to be selected for ministry.

The traditional dispensationalist argument that the gifts of apostle, prophet and evangelist died out at the end of the apostolic period tends therefore to be self-fulfilling. If these gifts are not valued, recognised or developed it is obvious that opportunities to express them atrophy. Despite this overwhelming tendency, it is abundantly clear that these gifts have not disappeared from the life of the church. Even a superficial glance at the various renewal movements in the church, whether we look at the monastic movements in the Catholic tradition or even movements which have courted heresy,[5] reveals that they have been led by those who have exhibited gifts which look remarkably like those of apostles, prophets and evangelists.

If we are not going to advocate "offices" in relation to these leadership gifts, how then do we describe the functioning of such gifts? From a practical perspective, an apostle is one who is able to begin significant new initiatives. That could be as local as a church plant or as widespread as a new movement within the church. Such people tend to embody that which they are proposing to begin before the actual structure comes into being. In an important sense they are that which they propose. In the case of a church plant, it is often the case that you could change everyone in the team and it would make little difference to the outcome except for that one person who clearly is the foundational leader, the one who is the church before it comes into being. Without that person the plant will not happen.

In this functional sense, a prophet is the kind of person who is able to "hear" or sense what God is doing in a given environment or situation. The ability to be sensitive to the activity of God is crucial in that it allows the new church or movement or initiative to cooperate with the Spirit of God who is already at work.

An evangelist is one who is able to communicate a sense of the love of God to those who stand on the edge or right outside of the orbit of God. It is just wonderful to watch a gifted evangelist building relationships with people and naturally sharing something of the reality of God with the people that she or he meets.

We could describe all three of these kinds of gifts as entrepreneurial in nature, but there is also a sense in which the combination of these giftings working together produces a keen sense of the presence and activity of God. In a book on the New Age Movement, the evangelist Rob Frost comments a number of times on the degree to which New Age adherents had begun their search for spirituality in the church as visitors or seekers, and had concluded that the God dimension was absent.[6] The operation of these kinds of gifts working in concert can have a dynamic impact on the God awareness of a Christian community.

If it is true that such gifts have never gone away, but have simply not been recognised, then we must ask the question, what has happened to the bearers of these gifts? The evidence suggests that they have not made it through denominational selection processes that are looking for pastor/teachers. Instead, there has been a tendency to move such people into missions, or into para-church agencies (often they have begun new ones) or, tragically, they have simply gone into the business world without seeing that activity as a valid ministry.

The situation of the post-Christendom church in the West demands that such people are recruited as a matter of urgency into ministry. If that is to happen, then not only will selection processes need to change but training will also need to change. More fundamentally still, our thinking about the nature of leadership and ministry will need to undergo a significant paradigm shift. It is not that the future mission church will no longer need pastors and teachers, but it will need them in dynamic team relationship with the other gifts.

3. Local Coalitions

There is a long and honourable tradition of churches cooperating with each other for evangelistic purposes. The most obvious example in the Western world relates to the frequent city-wide crusades most readily associated with evangelists such as Billy Graham. The core idea behind a large event relates not just to the quality of the event itself, but also to the attention that a high-profile location and celebrity can produce for the Christian community. Local churches simply cannot command that kind of attention for their own activity.

But the concept of coalition is increasingly being used much more widely than for the traditional evangelistic crusade. There are many examples of churches coming together to engage in social causes as well as for strategic church planting, in addition to a range of evangelistic initiatives that are not dependent on the single large event. The Alpha course would be one such example, alongside activities as diverse as city-wide prayer networks and events, work with teenagers over concentrated periods, schools initiatives, the mentoring of young people, educational workshops, initiatives with the unemployed, schemes to combat drug abuse, the rehabilitation of offenders and much more besides.

On occasion, Christian leaders across cities have sought to look strategically at the needs of a city in order to establish an overall plan that features both elements of social engagement and evangelistic enterprise. These are linked in the minds of those leaders as legitimate expressions of holistic mission. Often a wider plan begins with the building of strong relationships amongst clergy or sometimes youth workers. Prayer networks frequently emerge from these growing relationships of trust, and from prayer flows a determination to make a difference for the kingdom of God.

There is a twofold value in such united witness. First, it is undoubtedly the case that the wider society, particularly politicians, listen more carefully to a united witness than to the lobbying of a single church no matter if a mega church makes the approach. A cross-city initiative will almost always receive a better hearing than many approaches by individual churches.

Second, a united approach is always more effective even though it is often not possible to bring it into being. The task of reaching a whole city, or town or even region for the kingdom of God is huge when churches attempt to operate as single unconnected entities. The consequence of working together seems almost always to release gifts and resources. Whether in the field of training, planning or administration, there are often gifted individuals in local churches whose abilities are such that they are far more effective when operating on a larger stage. The fact of working together helps to release and involve lay people so that the church looks far more like a people movement than when we work as isolated units. The task is both too large and too important for us not to cooperate. The task of working together becomes more comprehensible when we understand the underlying nature of the mission of the church. It is to that core missionary understanding that we now turn.

NOTES

1. Hoke S Dickinson (Ed), *The Cane Ridge Reader*, Private Publication, 1972, p. 40f.

2. Herbert Schlossberg, *The Silent Revolution and the Making of Victorian England*, Ohio State University Press, 2000, p. 62ff.

3. For example, Michael Harper, *Let My People Grow: Ministry and Leadership in the Church*, Logos, 1977 and Arnold Bittlinger, *Gifts and Ministries*, Hodder and Stoughton, 1974.

4. There are some examples of such training but they tend to be either in the newly emerging churches in Africa, Asia and South America or amongst churches in the West that have large memberships drawn from such an ethnic constituency. They do not represent a mainstream or majority view within theological education.

5. For example, the Montanists from the early church or the Cathars from the medieval period.

6. Rob Frost, *A Closer Look at New Age Spirituality*, Kingsway, 2001, p. 109.

CHAPTER FIVE

THE CHURCH AND ITS MISSION

Looking at the soaring vaults of the great medieval cathedrals of Europe, it is clear that the church in the West has travelled a long journey since Christian missionaries in Ireland first erected the simple, windowless, stone, beehive huts which can still be seen on the Dingle peninsula. Hearing the magnificence of the cathedral's choral singing and the dignity of the liturgy led from the high altar it is all too easy to focus on that which is needed to maintain such splendour as compared with the purpose for which such effort was originally expended.

Nor is this merely a problem for the staff of the state church. All of us who are engaged in the service of the church are just as susceptible to being seduced by our own structures. Some commentators have summed up the private dream of all ministers as: more people, happy people, bigger budgets, more programmes. We may deny it if we like but few church leaders are immune to such temptation.

The realisation that I was not immune came to me some years ago. I can remember one of the pastorates that I had in my late 20s. I had come out of seminary believing that good preaching was good leadership. With that in mind I spent about 30 hours a week preparing the multiple messages that I needed to deliver every week. As I prepared my teaching, I sensed that God really spoke to me through the passages of scripture that I studied. We saw hundreds of new people come to that church in a short period of time. I remember sitting in my office one day thinking about all that was happening when two questions formed in my mind: "Where have all these people come from and what am I doing in the midst of all this?" The answer to the first was clear. Nearly all of these people had come from other good evangelical, orthodox, Bible-believing churches in the area. Why were they leaving their churches and coming to ours?

I had to face some painful truths. I would like to have claimed that it was happening because we taught God's truth or that God was at work in some powerful and remarkable way. But it was probably more realistic to recognise that a huge factor in the attraction of Christians from other churches was the platform performance. The pastors of the churches they were leaving were not less faithful but they just didn't have what we might call the "golden tongue" that produced an entertaining platform performance. There really wasn't a better reason than this. We were not more faithful, more true to scripture, more insightful or better servants of God than the leaders of the churches that they had left.

That was when I believe God said to me, "Dwight, do you think that my church is a warehouse which exists for the sole purpose of filling it with people to listen to you talk?" I remember thinking, "Well, God, yes, as a matter of fact that's exactly what I thought you wanted. Doesn't that make you happy? Aren't you overjoyed to see so many people sitting there listening to the truth of the scripture preached with power?"

For the very first time it dawned on me that perhaps that was not what made God happy, that just possibly, gathering people to sit and listen to somebody talk about the Bible was not the primary reason for the existence of the church, that more people, happy people, bigger budgets, more programmes might not be the main reason for the existence of the church. Success by numbers was seductive. That experience caused me to ask some fundamental questions about what God actually did want for his church.

My intentions were good but the basic mistake that I had made was to confuse the growth of numbers in the pew with the success of the mission of the church. That is not to say that the growth of the church might not be a good and desirable outcome of the success of the actual mission of the church but it is not and can never be the same thing as mission itself.

UNDERSTANDING AND ACCOMPLISHING THE PURPOSE OF THE CHURCH

So how might we understand the mission of the church in such a way that we can determine whether or not the true purpose of the church is being accomplished? The conviction of the first Christians, who did not have the New Testament to hand, was that the Old Testament gave a clear picture of the purpose of the church in terms of the fulfilment of the purpose of God for Israel. The people of Israel were not to exist for themselves but to be a light to the nations.[1]

The call to witness to all nations was clearly part of the ministry of Jesus, not in the sense that he had an active and sustained ministry to Gentiles but in the sense that he understood the call of Israel to minister to the Gentiles. Nowhere is that awareness more clear than in the anger that Christ turns towards the money changers. He was not angry that they were trading in the temple of God; in one sense they were only providing a necessary service. Their crime was not the making of money but the fact that they were doing so in the court of the Gentiles. This activity was excluding the very people for whom Israel had come into being. It is no accident that Jesus quotes from the prophet Isaiah. The full quotation points to the temple being a house of prayer for many nations. It is significant that Luke, with his special interest in the mission to the Gentiles, should be the only one of the writers of the synoptic gospels to feature this incident. John also refers to this incident at the beginning of his gospel but does not make the reference to Isaiah as explicitly as Luke does.[2]

Therefore, just as Israel was not to exist for its own sake but for the sake of the nations, so the church was to exist for the mission of God in the whole world. The concern for mission which binds both Old and New Testaments together is well expressed in the definition of mission arrived at by the Lambeth conference of 1988. It is sometimes referred to as the five marks of mission:

- To proclaim the good news of the gospel
- To teach, baptise and nurture new believers
- To respond to human need by loving service
- To seek to transform unjust structures of society
- To strive to safeguard the integrity of creation, to sustain and renew the life of the earth

Each of these marks points to the fact that mission is not evaluated first and foremost by the growth of the church either in numbers or in power and influence but primarily by the difference the church engaged in mission makes to the world. The addition of people into the church is first and foremost a work of the Lord of the harvest (Acts 2). The success of the institution must never be our focus but only the mission impact of what the institution of the church accomplishes.

If the church is merely the means by which mission takes place and mission is the end towards which the church should focus, why is it that Christians all too easily enter into such a ready confusion between ends and means? Part of the difficulty is that in all human enterprises ends and means are easily confused. While the difference between these two may be abundantly clear to visionary leaders, the demarcation is often more subtle than we may care to admit. How can we prise apart that subtlety to understand how God's purpose (mission) is often usurped by the means he has chosen (the church)?

The difficulty is well illustrated by looking at the very metaphors that the great missionary, St Paul, uses to describe the church. Four metaphors, all of which are used in Ephesians 2:19–22, serve to make the point.

First, the church is a nation of fellow citizens (see also 1 Corinthians 12:13 and Galatians 3:28). A character in the film *My Big Fat Greek Wedding* makes the observation, "There are two kinds of people in the world – those who are Greek and those who would like to be Greek." That very contemporary statement echoes a much older Greek view which divided the world into Greeks and barbarians. Jews saw themselves as a third race alongside the civilised mixture of Graeco-Roman culture and the barbarians beyond the empire. Paul suggests that Christians are a new race or nation that binds together members taken from all other nations on earth. This was not a nation with its own physical boundaries, but a wandering, alien people looking to heaven as their final home.

The later success of the church in converting the empire soon identified spiritual space with physical space. The empire was to be a Christian empire. It is only relatively recently that we have stopped thinking of the nations of the West as Christian nations. The state churches that grew up in Western nations have acted as powerful repositories for the myth of Christian nationhood. To refer again to the film *My Big Fat Greek Wedding*, when the prospective Anglo-Saxon bridegroom was baptised into the Greek Orthodox Church, the film makes it clear that he was not becoming a Christian; he was becoming Greek. The biblical metaphor of the church as a nation has all too often been usurped by the themes of Christendom which has tended to see the expansion of the church as the purpose of mission rather than the life of mission being the purpose of the church. In his book, *The Wound of Knowledge*, Rowan Williams writes of the tensions that the notion of "Christian empire" brought even as long ago as St Augustine's time. He points out that Augustine, author of the *City of God*, which apparently seeks to legitimise the concept of Christendom, died just as the barbarians were laying siege to his own city of Hippo.[3]

A second metaphor is that of a household or family (see also Romans 8:15, 1 Timothy 3:15 and Galatians 4:6). The intention of Paul is to use such a metaphor to emphasise the Fatherhood of God over all. We recognise our essential belonging as we begin to respond in faith – "Abba, Father!" The family in ancient times was a large and all-embracing idea. It did not just include mother, father and the children, but also included a wider circle of blood relations, servants, slaves and even those who had been adopted into a particular family. The head of the household offered a wide protection and sense of belonging. The boundaries had some fluidity. It does not take much imagination to see how the very personal concept of family, with its emphasis on familial relationship, can easily become an institutional notion. The household of God is easily identified with the much more static idea of a defined membership. Adding members is the modern measure of the church as compared with the more flexible metaphor of a wider familial embrace – the grace of the Father seeking long-lost family members.

A third metaphor is that of a building (see also 1 Peter 2:4). The New Testament concept of a building was very dynamic. Jesus was to be the cornerstone – a clear reference to the prophecy in Isaiah 28:16, and the foundations were to be the apostles and the prophets. Believers were seen as living stones, helping to construct a visible but very personal witness in the world. This notion of church was that of an idea or a construct which had an infectious impact on those who encountered it. The very nature of the church is constituted by the interconnectedness of each stone. Not only does each stone impact on the growing Christ-like quality of other stones through the interpersonal rub of relationships, but this interpersonal dynamic, lived out and in and among the world, becomes a primary sign of the fruit of the Spirit working in Christ's people. The extra-ordinariness of their everyday relationships in marriage, family and church body act as a compelling sign to others that the grave is indeed empty and that Christ "lives" in his people. They are the temple of the living God! The notion of "people" is the most basic and compelling first nature of the church. People in whom and through whom Christ lives and speaks to the nations.

Since Christians did not have church buildings, there was little danger of the church being identified with a physical structure. However, once church buildings became the norm, the term "church" and the idea of a church building became interchangeable to the point that for most people in the Western world a church is a building. Indeed to speak about the church as people seems to strike most of the population as a rather strange idea. To go further, for a church to meet somewhere other than in a recognisably church-shaped edifice sounds more like a sect or a cult. It is understandable as a temporary solution while a church building is acquired or built, but not to have a building at all seems strange to the point of being perverse.

Although committed Christians might be very familiar with the idea of the church as people and not primarily as an institution, it is worth reflecting that it is not so many years since such thinking was a rather novel idea for Christians as much as for the wider population. It is easier for those of us who know individuals who are the church to think of people before we think of structures, but even for us, the words "church" and "building" go very easily together.

The fourth metaphor is that of temple (see also 1 Corinthians 6:19). The first believers would have readily under-

stood the significance of the importance of the change of location of temple from the one in Jerusalem to the heart of every
follower of Jesus. The corporate nature of this relationship
derives its significance only from the primary residence of God
in Jesus' people as individuals. All of the Old Testament mean-
ings of temple are transferred to this new locality of God in
people. And, by extension, wherever they "go", God and his
revelation goes. Whereas, in the Old Testament there is a call to
the nations to focus their attention on Jerusalem and on what
God is going to do there, in the New Testament believers carry
the witness about God and his message out to the nations.

For Jewish believers, the temple was the place where God
especially dwelt. We can assume that by the time Paul had written to the Ephesians, the story of how the curtain in the holy of
holies was torn at the time of the death of Christ was well
known. God's presence was now released in a new way. God no
longer inhabited a particular place, such as the temple, but he
was present in a powerful way wherever the new people of
God, the church, gathered or went. The miraculous deeds of
God, healings, exorcisms, speaking in tongues and interpretations, prophetic utterances and many other answered prayers
all demonstrate that God released his presence into the world
through Christ's people. The Spirit of God was clearly present
in ways that were demonstrably visible for those with eyes to
see and ears to hear.

The first flush of Pentecostal enthusiasm did not last indefi-
nitely. As time went on, the evidence of healing and the miraculous diminished. Arguably, the mysteries of the Eucharist,
enhanced by liturgical form, and eventually given shape by
buildings that could be thought of as temples of worship,
replaced the more spontaneous forms of worship that predom-
inated amongst the early converts. Regular public worship
requires a professional clergy, and inevitably, professional
clergy, together with permanent buildings, require financial
resource. It is not difficult to see how the emphasis on mission

began to shift towards the preservation of emerging structures and so to maintenance. With this transference, the significance of God released in and through each of Christ's people is lost. The world is asked to come and see, rather than the church going, living and telling in and through all of its normal daily activities and relationships. What had been designed by God, and empowered by the Spirit to be in the world, becomes locked away in place and programme.

THE PURPOSE OF GOD

How can we then prevent ourselves and each other from slipping so easily from a concern for mission (ends) to a preoccupation with church (the means)? Certain key principles need to be captured and integrated. These principles can be clearly seen in Paul's letter to the Ephesians in chapter 3:10–11. It is with great thankfulness that we receive these words, for their precise relationship and application are found nowhere else in the New Testament. Without this idea, so powerfully expressed by Paul in this passage, our understanding of the role of the church in the world would be clouded.

Ephesians 3:10–11 frames the essence of a biblical ecclesiology that every 1st century Christian would have understood without thinking. It is to this simplicity of nature that we need to be restored.

His intent was that now, through the church, the manifold wisdom of God should be made known to the rulers and authorities in the heavenly realms, according to his eternal purpose which he accomplished in Christ Jesus our Lord (Ephesians 3:10–11).

Four key elements emerge.

First, God has a single eternal purpose. Possibly the most remarkable aspect of the Bible is that these 66 books tell one story. Certainly it is gathered into two testaments – old and new, but there is only one story. We need both testaments because the Old Testament can only be properly understood in terms of its fulfilment in the New Testament and because the New Testament is properly illumined by the light of the Old Testament. But whether we are reading the Old or the New Testament, there is essentially only one story amongst the many stories.

What is that story? It is the story of how God is both Creator and Father of us all. It is the story of a world that, having been made by God and endued with freedom, chooses evil. That choice of evil fractures the universe and spoils what God had intended. However, God always had a plan and that involved the sending of his Son, Jesus Christ, to reconcile the whole of creation to God, to heal and restore that which is damaged until God's original purpose for his world is recovered. The particular story of Israel, of the coming of the Messiah and the creation of the church are all chapters in an emerging single story.

The calling into being of Israel and the arrival of Jesus are not afterthoughts but were always present as possibilities from the beginning. The nature of God is to both create and to be a Father. He has created, not just a beautiful world, but a personal world in which human beings reflect his image and can be known personally and know him personally. That central purpose of God has remained unchanged since the beginning of time and will remain unchanged until the end of time.

Along the way, God has other concerns. He is concerned for the poor, for the weak and for the helpless. He is a God of justice and so the agenda in pursuit of the core purpose may well be long and complex on occasion. But the core purpose never changes.

Second, for this time and place, the church is God's chosen instrument. The church in the Western world has received an extremely bad press during the first few years of the 21st century. Even those parts of the church which had seemed to weather the storm better than others, for example the Roman Catholic Church in places such as Ireland and the United States, have received a very severe blow to their moral authority as the scandal of paedophile priests has gradually been uncovered. Clergy who once enjoyed a position of some standing in society are no longer viewed as worthwhile contributors to serious moral debate about the future of society. With some notable exceptions, the views of church leaders are not usually eagerly sought out by politicians, either locally or nationally. There are few leaders in the Western church that enjoy the same influence as figures such as Desmond Tutu in South Africa.

As church life has moved to the periphery of the broader society, many who describe themselves as believers have moved beyond the doors of the church. Some are simply alienated by what they perceive as a lack of spiritual life within the church; others have concluded that the church serves no useful purpose and that they can manage busy lives without the additional pressures that involvement in a church can bring.

Alan Jamieson in his book *A Churchless Faith*[4] describes in some detail the journey of the disillusioned as they gradually question their involvement in the church and begin a process of withdrawal. For some, it is simply boredom. There seems to be an absence of a compelling vision that induces either enthusiasm or commitment. For others the process begins with a specific incident which results in hurt; for yet others it is a disillusionment that arises from a realisation that the lofty ideals preached earnestly from the pulpit are not necessarily reflected in the reality of a church community, particularly church communities which are feeling dispirited and even threatened by their isolation in broader society. Clearly, there are many who attempt to live out their faith without any reference to the Christian church.

It is not the purpose of this book to denigrate the efforts of those who attempt to reflect the values of the kingdom of God through their lives outside of the structures of the church. It is also important to recognise that there are also many who would not call themselves Christians who are working for social justice in such a way that their activity can be admired by Christians. We might even want to be inspired by such people to engage in similar activities. These efforts are all commendable. But, having said all that, the scriptures constantly remind us that whatever we might think of the church, God still loves the church.

Not only does scripture give ample testimony to God's loving care for the church; at no point is there any suggestion that there might be another plan. The church is called to be a partner in the mission of God and as far as we can tell he has not changed his mind. Despite all of its faults, failures, disobedience and weakness, the church remains the imperfect vessel through which God intends to work out his plan of reconciliation for mankind. That does not mean that God is not active outside of the church. Plainly the Holy Spirit goes ahead of the church. But the Spirit is not preparing the way for another agency. The Holy Spirit's work is entirely consistent with the work of the Father and the Son.

Church history reminds us that the church requires renewal from time to time in order to engage adequately in its calling, but the calling never changes. The renewal of the church is not for the sake of the church but for the sake of the mission of the church. And so, we need a restoration to an old deep-seated conviction, but new to us. Whatever God is going to do in the world, he is going to do through all of Christ's people. That is not to say that God cannot or does not move with anything less. But both scripture and history declare that the power of God in the gospel moves most effectively when the greatest majority of the followers of Jesus are releasing him into their everyday lives and relationships.

Third, every person in the church is a unique, unrepeated

and eternal part of God's grace story. Whenever the church stands in need of renewal, the cry for better leadership inevitably comes to the fore. Much of the secular criticism of the church is in fact aimed at its leaders. The focus on leadership is entirely understandable and appropriate. The church needs quality leadership even more acutely at times of crisis than when all seems well. But we must never lose sight of the objective of good leadership. The purpose of leadership is never to celebrate leadership itself. Rather, the goal of good leaders is to bring the whole membership of the body of Christ to the maturity of its purpose.

Paul, writing in Ephesians about leadership, reminds us that the purpose of leadership gifts is:

> . . . to prepare God's people for works of service, so that the body of Christ may be built up until we all reach unity in the faith and in the knowledge of the Son of God and become mature, attaining to the whole measure of the fullness of Christ (Ephesians 4:12, 13.)

The emphasis on the preparation of all of God's people is noticeable and continues through the remainder of Ephesians. It is not just leaders who are to do the work of God, but every member working together with leadership to fulfil the calling that comes from God for the whole church. The success or otherwise of leaders in mobilising the giftedness of the whole church is the single biggest factor in determining the effectiveness of the church in mission. A Church of Scotland report, entitled *Church Without Walls*, indicates that the aim of the Special Commission that produced the report was " . . . to return the ministry of the Gospel to the people of God".[5]

It is no coincidence that growing churches, growing denominations and growing movements within Christianity share this common feature. Yes, prayer is important, certainly evangelistic endeavour matters, undoubtedly inspiring worship helps but all of these factors (and many more) are much more potent when every member is motivated to prayer, to evangelise and to share in worship as compared with the active minority.

Christianity grew in the first few centuries, not through the effectiveness of a professional leadership, but by the patient, consistent witness of ordinary traders, soldiers, civil servants and slaves, who carried the faith with them wherever they travelled in the world. The equipping of the saints to be active participants in the mission of God is a primary principle of mission.

Fourth, this grace story reworks the universe for eternity. Philip Yancey, in his best-selling book, *What's so Amazing about Grace?*, proceeds to answer his own question with story after story of how the exercise of grace created new personal paradigms for those who were infected by its surprising generosity. Acts of unexpected kindness that broke the normal rules of human interaction broke through hard hearts to change situations.

On the day after the first free elections for people of every race brought a new government to power in South Africa, a BBC reporter who was on the ground was asked by the presenter in London why there had not been the predicted bloodbath in that land. The reporter replied that he could only describe the amazing capacity of black South Africans to exercise Christian love and so to forgive. Grace can change the expected course of human history.

In the same way, Yancey also describes how the absence of grace sometimes shames the church and contradicts the core message of the gospel which is fundamentally a message of hope about the capacity of grace to reorder the world. The absence of grace is one of the themes of Alan Jamieson's book, mentioned above, as he describes the experiences of those who leave the church.

One of the great missionary stories of our age, the expansion of Baptist and Pentecostal churches in present-day Ukraine, underscores the place of compassionate mission. The church in Ukraine has a vision to plant 28,000 churches by the year 2015. They have already planted more than 6,000 churches as part of that endeavour. Their favoured approach to church planting is to find ways of meeting the human need of those who live in the cities where they plan to evangelise. Before grace is preached it is first practised, with astonishing consequences.

The multiple acts of grace that rework the universe are not necessarily the acts of the famous, though interestingly it is acts of grace that caused Mother Teresa to become someone who won worldwide admiration. Almost by definition, the acts of grace that most change the world consist of those actions that will never be widely publicised. They are the stories of the changed lives of very ordinary people.

No matter where in the world you look, those who have become Christians have overwhelmingly made such a decision because of the actions of ordinary people in their circle of influence. These ordinary people are not going to influence the lives of thousands of people but there are some people that they have a particular connection with who may listen to no one else. In a very particular and unique way they are strategically positioned in relation to some people.

It is when the church is able to mobilise the large majority of its membership such that these participants begin to see their lives as unique receivers and givers of grace that the church begins to take on the character of that which it has been called by God to be. It is the ordinary made extraordinary by virtue of a connection with the grace of God.

A Church of Scotland report put it this way:

The fundamental shift of mindset for the whole culture of the church is towards living out the cycle of grace in every relationship. Living out that spirituality of grace lies at the heart of the core calling to "follow me".[6]

NOTES

1. See for example Isaiah 42:6.
2. Luke 19:45, 46.
3. Rowan Williams, *The Wound of Knowledge*, DLT, 1979, p. 92.
4. Alan Jamieson, *A Churchless Faith*, Philip Garside Publishing, 2000, see especially pp. 53ff.
5. The General Assembly of the Church of Scotland Report, The Report of the Special Commission anent *(sic)* Review and Reform, *Church Without Walls*, p. 7.
6. Ibid., p. 19.

CHAPTER SIX

CHANGING THE PARADIGM

We are bound to ask the question: what would the church look like if it really did live out the grace stories of its members? Those of us who live as Christians in the Western world at the beginning of the 21st century are aware that dramatic change would be required of the church to allow that to happen. That change is sufficiently great that it constitutes the creation of a new paradigm – a completely new way of imagining the church.

Those who write about the shift from one paradigm to another are acutely aware that change of this order is very hard to bring about. Once the new paradigm is the norm, and everyone is used to dealing with it, experiencing it, learning it and observing it, then, just because it is the new nature of reality, everyone can be comfortable with the new. It is no longer the new – it is simply the way things are. But living between paradigms is hard. The new which is being born is not well known and it is all too easy to slip back into the paradigm with which we are familiar. Some refer to this as the default position.

What is the present familiar paradigm or default position? The Church of Scotland report cited in the previous chapter expresses the old (or possibly present) paradigm in these terms:

107

The Church of Scotland mission strategy is based on the 19th Century mission model: one minister in one building in one parish. All the resources of the uniting church of 1929 were harnessed to servicing this strategy.

As we enter the 21st Century, the emerging pattern for mission strategy must be much more diverse to permeate the fragmented nature of our society: ministry teams operating in a variety of community bases to be incarnated in a network of communities. Instead of occasional variations to the assumed 19th Century norm, it is time to recognize the new components of the new strategy and resource it accordingly.[1]

We can summarise the existing paradigm as one which centres on the minister (usually one with the gifts of pastor/teacher) as having a territorial emphasis (the parish or the community), and which sees the church as an organisation or institution. Such a model encourages us to think in terms of serving the church, whether as professional clergy or as lay people. The church is the focus of our concern and activity. The growth or otherwise of the church is the key measurement of success. Evangelistic strategy is concerned with how we bring people to church. Commitment to Jesus Christ is necessary because it is part of the package that enables us to join the church. A good result is that those who are drawn to the church become committed to the doctrine we espouse, but even more importantly, they join the church as active participants.

We are familiar with the paradigm, and in a situation where the predominant worldview was that of Christianity it was a paradigm that had much to commend it. In such a world it was not necessary to convince people of the truth of Christianity and the value of the church. These elements could at one time be assumed as the norm. The priority was to encourage people to have an active affiliation, meaningfully to express their dormant belief system. In such a situation, the structure of one minister in one building in one parish was an effective methodology to secure the presence of the church as an agent for good within reach of every person.

But even as the 19th century was drawing to a close, the challenge to Christianity as the primary worldview, or sacred canopy as Peter Berger calls it, was sufficiently great that some were seeing that change was necessary if the church was to be true to its calling. Missionary pioneers, notably Roland Allen, drawing on their experience of the mission field in Asia and Africa, began to speak of the need for a church of the laity. Allen's three-self concept of the church (self-governing, self-financing, self-reproducing) was possibly the first attempt by a Western church leader to begin to articulate a missionary model for the church in the 21st century.

But even Allen's radical thinking does not describe the paradigm shift that is necessary to construct an effective missionary church for our present time. Nor does the Church of Scotland document quoted above. Helpful though it is to talk of a shift to diverse models in order to permeate society, the parish model still looms over such talk as the dominant model which will always strive to reassert itself. The default position of the church is always that of the church as an institution.

The new paradigm, a missionary paradigm that beckons to us, necessitates a shift from institution to movement, from structures that invite people into sacred space to an infectious spirituality that invades secular space. The idea is not so hard to express, describe and grasp. The difficulty arises in actually living the paradigm because the old one constantly draws us back. All too often the best we can manage are initiatives that come out of the old paradigm and allow us to live in the new paradigm for while. Constructing a new model, which we live within as a permanent reality, is much more difficult.

How can we begin to create the new paradigm as more than just a fleeting experience? All too often we are tempted to look for structures that will replace the previous structures. There is some validity in doing so, and certainly it can be helpful to point to examples of new structures so that we can give shape and identity to the new. But before we talk of new structures it is vital to talk of the underpinning life which must be present if we are to prevent creative initiatives from becoming undermined by the paradigm of the past. What might those living realities be and how might we know if they are present?

1. Personal Transformation

Leaders in a new missionary paradigm are not looking to inspire willing followers, but rather to develop disciples with their own internal motivation. True motivation to become devoted followers of Jesus Christ begins from within and can never be imposed from without.

The power of testimony, of changed lives, is well attested within the Christian tradition. But the problem of developing a spirituality that lasts for the long haul is much more complex than producing initial enthusiasm. Failure to do so is costly and can result in many painful situations where those who still believe find themselves on an exit path out of church as part of a pilgrimage to find a meaningful spirituality.

In his book, *A Churchless Faith*, Alan Jamieson tells the stories of those whose spiritual experience has been in conflict with the churches they have inhabited. His study reveals that the problem of church leavers is particularly acute for the very churches that are most adept at attracting new worshippers. He calls them the EPC churches by which he means Evangelical, Pentecostal and Charismatic churches. [2] Some of those who arrive in EPC churches have previously been members of one or other of the historic churches and move to an EPC church because of the perception that they are more lively, more relevant, more committed and more enthusiastic than the historic churches. But lively worship is not enough by itself to sustain personal transformation.

Jamieson's accounts of the struggles of church leavers

suggests that lively worship acts more as an agent of transfusion than transformation. It is as if the worship experience functions as a substitute for a well-developed personal spirituality and tends towards dependency or a consumerist approach to worship. Some of those who left such churches include on occasion the leaders themselves and the reasons they give relate to the feeling that there is a divide between the sacred and the secular. In such a system the sacred represents a refuge from the secular as compared with a resource from which to inhabit the secular.

Rob Frost, a Christian leader amongst British evangelicals, describes similar feelings in his book *A Closer Look at New Age Spirituality*. He says of himself:

> To be frank, I am deeply disillusioned with what the church is offering Sunday by Sunday. There is a deadness in the ritual, a dryness in the formality, and a growing irrelevance in the institution.[3]

We are bound to ask: what would it look like for a church to function in such a way that the goal of church life was not merely to attract more people into membership and attendance but to produce people that had a profound sense of their personal relationship to God, resource in Christ, and could take that reality into the world with them?

Evangelicals have traditionally emphasised personal Bible reading, and personal quiet times in which both to speak to God and to listen to God. This is not the only model in which personal spirituality can be developed, but more important than the precise model is the process by which Christians are encouraged to develop a profound awareness of the presence of God in their lives. Few churches have any way of measuring their effectiveness in producing such personal transformation in their members and adherents. More particularly, few church leaders are skilled in empowering individuals towards authentic spirituality. The experience of weekly worship together with weekly preaching and teaching are not known as effective models for encouraging personal transformation. There is a need for the measured development of intimacy with God in the lives of every Christian.

The natural context for the fostering of such intimacy is that of the small group. Fortunately, many churches in the West do have a pattern of small groups as a regular feature of church life, but the question remains: what happens in such groups? Suppose that churches used their small group structure as places where intentional mentoring took place designed to develop personal transformation. Regardless of the precise paradigm of church that particular ages have used, the transmission of the faith through some kind of mentoring system has always been essential.

For the Methodist revival of the late 18th and early 19th century, it was the class system that stood at the centre of that genuine people movement. Recently I read an unpublished manuscript written by a Methodist convert in the early years of the 19th century. The manuscript had been handed down through the family. It portrays a picture of personal transformation. In pages of handwritten testimony, the convert in question describes the moment of his conversion, the immediate consequences and then his growth in faith. At no point does he describe a worship service or refer to a clergyman. His conversion and subsequent mentoring all took place through a network of lay people in the context of personal conversations and small group meetings.

Whatever the age, four measures of personal transformation are possible.

i. A knowledge of God through the scriptures

We could go further and talk of falling in love with God through the powerful pictures of God transmitted through scripture stories. All the current evidence indicates that the scriptures are being read less and less even by evangelical Christians. Scripture represents a powerful resource for the imagination of the follower of Christ. The Bible Society in many countries has promoted a programme called "Faith Comes by Hearing". The programme consists of audio tapes of the whole New Testament. Congregations are challenged to encourage as many people as possible to listen to the New Testament on their own set of tapes and to follow the programme over a set 40-day period. The mutual encouragement of doing so as a part of a church experience encourages high levels of participation.

Research conducted in churches that had used the programme produced some fascinating results. First, even those Christians who thought they knew the scriptures well began to realise that they had never engaged much with whole stories so much as with short texts. A good number of participants had to check their Bibles to make sure that what they were hearing was actually in the scripture. They consistently found that they were discovering the Bible afresh. Second, clergy often reported that the experience helped in the spiritual formation of the congregation. Third, many church leaders noted a growth in the number of Christians offering themselves for service in the church at the conclusion of the programme.

Small groups are places in which Christians can be encouraged to re-engage with the Bible such that the core stories become well known. You might ask yourself, if you had the opportunity to teach no more than 24 stories from the scripture to a new convert who knew none at all, what would they be? Would it be possible to ensure that everyone in your congregation had a deep knowledge of at least those 24 stories?

ii. Listening to God

The notion that God can speak to us is sometimes interpreted as close to religious mania or even to mental ill health. Yet how is it possible to have any sense of maturity in the Christian faith without seeing followers of Jesus recognising the authentic voice of God in their lives? Such a recognition of the still quiet voice of God who helps us to see "this is the way, walk in it" can be taught. The alternative to not teaching believers how to have a healthy listening ear tends to produce either the disuse or misuse of guidance – spiritual indolence or spiritual arrogance.

We may not all become mystics in the desert, but for our own spiritual well-being we should at least be able to find our own places of retreat and calm so that we can then engage wholeheartedly in the storms of life. Listening to the guidance of God helps us to give meaning and value to our life experiences. Once again, the intimacy of the small group offers a context for exploration and experimentation in the discipline of spiritual listening.

iii. Personal relationships

Those who are leaders in church life are all too aware of the fact that significant numbers of people react to conflict by leaving the church. One researcher who has written extensively on congregational transformation has said rather starkly, "Our congregations, whatever else they are, are seething pools of conflict."[4] There is a good deal of evidence to suggest that some of those who leave because of conflict, attend other churches where eventually the same process is repeated. Such individuals may try a number of churches before deciding not to attend any church at all. The key problem is that no one ever took the trouble to equip them to deal with conflict in the body of Christ. Interestingly, the problem is dealt with very clearly in the scriptures. The New Testament is very realistic about the reality of conflict in the church. And so it should be because conflict is a normal part of the human condition. We cannot avoid it but we can learn to use it to provoke personal growth.

In light of the picture we saw in Ephesians 2:19–22, preparing believers to see conflict as an opportunity for growth and not as a tragedy to avoid at all costs, is part of the maturation process necessary for personal transformation. Love does not seek to avoid conflict at any price any more than it seeks to promote it. The grace of God living in us seeks to produce communities that become healthy places to be because individuals learn to relate well to one another. Believers learn to live in mutual forgiveness, understanding and encouragement – to produce what the clinical psychologist, Frank Lake, once called the "cycle of grace", as a way of describing healthy human development.

iv. Using our giftedness

Over the last 20 years, church growth literature has abounded in books that urge congregations to release the gifts of every member. Congregations such as Willow Creek Community Church have even published materials that are designed to help identify the gifts of church members. The reason for this emphasis is not difficult to see. It is obvious that growing churches have a mobilised membership. The key to the mobilisation of significant numbers of church members does not lie in sermons designed to emphasise commitment accompanied by frequent exhortations to become involved. Members become mobilised when their internal motivations are recognised and used. This is a key element in personal transformation. Personal motivation is intimately connected to the gifts that people have within them.

But there is a problem with such an approach. It is one thing to recognise giftedness; it is quite another to relate such discovery to actual opportunities to serve. It is at this point that many congregations fail to use the real benefit in gift identification exercises. There are not a few churches that have used gift discovery processes but tend to see them as an end in themselves. The truth is that many churches are not structured in such a way that they can offer ministries to those whose gifts become clear. There is a limit to the number of gifts that are required in congregations which are maintenance orientated. How many people do you really require to operate a congregation which intends to keep everything running as it has always operated? Not too many! To use the gifts of every member requires a church to structure its life around mission. Once that has happened there is no limit to the number of gifts that can be used.

Such congregational transformation cannot happen overnight. There is a need for churches to begin processes that begin to match the development of a missionary ethos to the development of every-member ministry. Gift discovery exercises allow congregations to connect mission to ministry. The identification of gifts with no opportunity to serve acts as a recipe for frustration and the possible exit of those who have discovered their gift but have no outlet for service.[5]

2. Genuine Diversity in Leadership

Leadership is the key to much that we have described above but it is also an area of real challenge. The last 20 years have witnessed a mushrooming of literature on the issue of leadership, particularly in the world of business. The last decade of the previous century saw a shift from a concern for management to that of leadership. One writer on leadership put it this way:

A couple of years ago when passing through Los Angeles I picked a newspaper off the airport bookstand. In it was a report of a conference of trustees and managers from more than 1,000 of America's most elite institutions, the group of large philanthropic foundations whose purpose is to give away money. The theme of their three-day conference was "Exploring the many dimensions of leadership".

The conclusions the conference came to were startling. There was, they agreed, nothing less than a crisis of leadership in American society; the nation was being guided, not by leaders but by managers and its condition could be described as being over-managed and under-led![6]

The response of business to the issue of leadership has sometimes been to highlight the achievements of exceptional leaders, especially those who have led from the front. The underlying suggestion is that we can all be great leaders if only we learn the principles of leadership. Sober reflection reveals that life is more complex. In reality, no matter what some exceptional entrepreneurs may have achieved, there are different kinds of leaders. Moreover, all leaders need some kind of team if they are going to achieve much within any organisation.

More recently, organisations have begun to speak about flat structures in which leadership is exercised through teams. The revolt against hierarchies that stress the role of one dominant leader is pronounced and noticeable amongst Generation Xers. One Christian website, <postmission.com>, which describes itself as an international forum on Christian mission in post-modernity, raised the issue of leadership above every other question. A common theme throughout the chat room is the rejection of "domineering" leaders – those who seek to control, to emphasise their authority, and to exercise power in ways that demanded obedience simply because the person issuing the dictates is the leader.

Probably the most disturbing aspect of the discussion on the website and indeed in a survey of Christian literature is the tendency for Christian leaders to look to the secular spheres of business and politics for models of good leadership. Ironically some of the best literature on leadership in the secular sphere talks about leadership in ways that are deeply reminiscent of scripture. There has come a growing realisation that one of the key ingredients in leadership is that of character. You can't get much more scriptural than that! Indeed one business school has even conducted research on leadership and spirituality.

But the reality remains that many churches have had difficulty in constructing teams of diversely gifted people that work. Genuine mutuality in leadership is acknowledged as present in scripture but churches find it hard to work out on the ground. To an extent, the difficulty lies in the fact that we stand between paradigms. The old paradigm, one minister, in one building in one parish, is very hard to leave behind. Sometimes we have updated the paradigm to read, one very successful minister with a large staff in a huge church relating to an area of a city, but basically it is the same paradigm.

The modification of the paradigm to include "success" is sometimes given a spiritual veneer by talk of an "anointed" leader, regardless of the fact that such anointing in the context of leadership is more commonly an Old Testament concept – before the Spirit was poured out on all believers. Sharing power, acknowledging the gifts of others, celebrating the achievements of others is a harder paradigm to grasp, in part because the new structures to express a new paradigm are still in the process of being invented. But the mandate for such leadership is clearly present in scripture.

> Jesus called them together and said, "You know that the rulers of the Gentiles lord it over them, and their high officials exercise authority over them. Not so with you. Instead, whoever want to become great among you must be your servant, and whoever wants to be first must be your slave – just as the Son of Man did not come to be served, but to serve, and to give his life as a ransom for many" (Matthew 20:25–28).

We will discuss in a later chapter the requirements of leadership, especially in relation to team. For the moment it is enough to acknowledge that the creation of mutuality in leadership, the formation of satisfying, effective teams is a critical ingredient. We can hardly expect church members to exercise grace, to build one another up, if they rarely witness a depth of relationship emanating from the leadership team. To accomplish a depth of relationship not only means spending time with one another, sometimes at the expense of the task, but it also means developing significant self-awareness. Seeing ourselves as we really are can be painful especially if such self-knowledge collides with unrealistic aspirations.

3. Creating Organic Movement

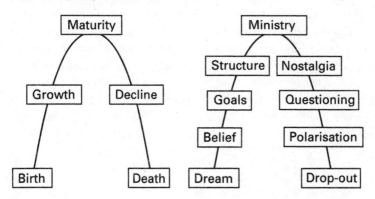

[7]The traditional bell curve serves to highlight two realities which exist in tension when we consider movements of any kind, namely, the tension between means (organisation) and ends (purpose). The early phases of any movement are highly organic. In other words they tend to have a large measure of spontaneous growth and are very light on organisation. Ironically the time when a movement expands at the most rapid rate is the moment when it matures sufficiently to have the resources to organise. Organisation adds enormous power to organic movement.

Once an organisation has reached the point of plateau, the tendency is for the means to become confused with the ends. The organisation and its survival is seen by the leaders as more important than the mission. The greater the organisational crisis, the less attention is paid to the original purpose or mission. We will leave you to decide where on the bell curve the church in the West might be placed. But if the church is to be renewed, it is essential for it to recover both a vision for its original purpose and a degree of spontaneous and organic growth.

The problem with spontaneous movements is that by definition you cannot organise them into being. The missiologist Andrew Walls describes the origins of a number of spontaneous people movements in West Africa. One illustration taken from the many that he offers makes the point:

The Methodist Church in Ashanti, Ghana, owes much to the preaching of a charismatic jailbird called Sampson Oppong. Oppong always claimed that he had little knowledge of Christianity at all before his call as a preacher. The dramatic events that led up to his entry on his vocation included a prophetic dream and its fulfillment the next day, an attempt to poison a Christian that failed because the intended victim vomited the substance after saying grace, and an alcoholic stupor during which Oppong was punitively kicked by a sheep he had stolen. The Methodist mission estimated that as a result of this man's preaching, twenty thousand people came under their pastoral care within five or six years.[8]

It would be difficult to form a mission model either from the story of Oppong or indeed from hundreds of other stories of spontaneous growth. However, there are some common themes in the growth of all movements. First, someone (or some people) have experienced the grace of God in a sufficiently life-changing way that they have felt compelled to communicate it to others. Second, they have been able to imagine and express this experience in clothing that fits their audience. Third, someone (and it may not be the initiator) has recognised the significance of events and has provided some organisational structure.

The difficulty for the church in the West is that we have considerable organisational ability but little that is organic and spontaneous to organise. The gifts we currently need relate to the sowing of many seeds amongst diverse people groups and waiting to see what happens. Discipling, equipping and releasing those who have had significant grace experiences and who have the desire and ability to communicate needs to be the priority for the moment. Insisting that such disciples bring the fruit of their work into existing structures will almost certainly stop spontaneous growth from taking place. We need to be willing to birth the new with a spirit of generosity.

4. The Church as a Dispersed Presence

This all points to the necessity to see the church as a dispersed presence in the world in at least equal measure to the notion of a gathered centre. The concept of the church as individuals that witness to a measure of grace wherever they work and live as advocates for a powerful message is an idea that strikes most Christians as far from reality. It is only just about possible to envisage the idea of Christians inviting others to come to church as a central gathering. Of course the two ideas are not mutually exclusive but to change the weight of emphasis from gathering to dispersion suggests that new habits are formed.

What might these new habits be? Listening to the needs of others, expressing care and concern, offering prayer and bringing the God dimension to bear into a myriad of human situations represents a beginning. Christians normally do not feel confident to engage in such activity. This is as much because of the secularisation of society as it is due to any lack of faith in the lives of ordinary believers. The absence of a God-soaked consciousness in Western society has made it difficult in the past for people to speak of a spiritual dimension to life without appearing to be strange in some way. God and his perspective are not often on the agenda for most people to talk about.

Those who have lived in other parts of the world notice the ease with which most cultures do bring the eternal, the spiritual, the divine, into everyday life and conversation. For most peoples around the globe, prayer is a very natural expression of living. Western secular society represents a strange exception to the norm of human experience. The process of secularisation teaches (and almost enforces) a construct that causes the natural God-consciousness of children to be suppressed and buried so that adults, brought up in such a system, are far less aware of the spiritual issues in life than they might otherwise be.

The impact of secularisation is reinforced by unfavourable stereotypes of Christians in the media. Mark Greene, writing in *Thank God it's Monday*, says of Christians:

> Christians don't have a very good image. On TV, clergy are often portrayed as well-meaning, bumbling, absent-minded, slightly overweight, giggly wimps with secret weaknesses for sherry or cream cakes. The reality of the non-Christian's view is probably bleaker. Who, for example, is describing whom in these research results?
>
> These people are . . .

> Less free
> More unfashionable
> More isolated
> Less sexually fulfilled
> More boring
> Psychologically weaker
> With fewer interests
> Less realistic
> Less involved in the real world
> Less happy
> Less friendly . . .

> That's the opinion of Newcastle students about Christians.[9]

However, there is a growing body of evidence to suggest that such a situation is rapidly changing.

*University of Nottingham: The Spiritual Life of People
Who Don't Go to Church*[10]

Table 2: FREQUENCY OF REPORT OF RELIGIOUS OR SPIRITUAL EXPERIENCE IN BRITAIN FOR THE YEARS 1987 AND 2000		
	1987	**2000**
A patterning of events	29%	55%
Awareness of the presence of God	27%	38%
Awareness of prayer being answered	25%	37%
Awareness of a sacred presence in nature	16%	29%
Awareness of the presence of the dead	18%	25%
Awareness of an evil presence	12%	25%
*CUMULATIVE TOTAL	48%	76%

*This includes totals for respondents to two additional questions asked in 1987 about "a presence not called God" (22%) and "awareness that all things are One" (5%), i.e. the total of 76% for the year 2000 is quite likely to be relatively speaking an underestimate.

Anecdotal evidence gained from many conversations with Christians who are lay people, as well as with clergy, suggests that the formal research conducted by David Hay is borne out by experience. There could well be a change coming with growing opportunity for Christians to gain a new confidence in talking about spiritual experiences, offering prayer and even seeing miracles take place outside of the circle of Sunday worship. One church in Britain recently attended a New Age fair, offering to talk to people about Christianity, giving away literature and offering prayer. They reported a surprising number of positive conversations with those who attended. The spiritual climate is changing; the church needs to be gearing up to be a dispersed presence.

NOTES

1. The General Assembly of the Church of Scotland Report, The Report of the Special Commission anent Review and Reform, *Church Without Walls*, p. 14.
2. Alan Jamieson, *A Churchless Faith*, Philip Garside Publishing, 2000, p. 16.
3. Rob Frost, *A Closer Look at New Age Spirituality*, Kingsway, 2001, p. 9.
4. Loren Mead, *Transforming Congregations for the Future*, Alban Institute, 1994, p. 49.
5. Henri Nouwen, *The Wounded Healer*, DLT, 1979, p. 42.
6. Tom Marshall, *Understanding Leadership*, Sovereign World International, 1991, p. 5.
7. Robert Dale, *To Dream Again: How to Help Your Church Come Alive*, Broadman Press, 1981, pp. 15 and 17.
8. Andrew Walls, *The Missionary Movement in Christian History*, T and T Clark, 1996, p. 88.
9. Mark Greene, *Thank God it's Monday*, Scripture Union, p. 43f.
10. David Hay and Kate Hunt, *Understanding the Spirituality of People Who Don't Go to Church*, A Report on the Findings of the Adult's Spirituality Project at the University of Nottingham, 2000, p. 13.

CHAPTER SEVEN

ALONE AT THE TOP: THE CREATION OF A LEADERSHIP CULTURE

In the previous chapter we commented on the extent to which we define leadership in terms of a few exceptional leaders. This is true both in the business and in the church world. Increasingly, we are beginning to see the limitations even of exceptional individual leadership. In the book on business excellence, *Built to Last*, the writers comment on the role of some of the best known individuals in American industry. One of those individuals is Jack Welch of the General Electric Company. They make the telling point that the long-term culture of the organisation is as important as the remarkable individual. They say this:

> We respect Welch for his remarkable track record. But we respect GE even more for its remarkable track record of continuity in top management excellence over the course of a hundred years.[1]

What individual can claim credit for 100 years of success? The creation of a nourishing culture in which good leadership can be fostered and developed is clearly a critical ingredient in institutions which last. Institutions of this kind are not static monoliths, but flexible and creative structures which have learnt how to renew their life and energy on a regular basis. So what is it that stops the creation of such an environment?

Robert Greenleaf, commenting upon the failure of today's Western organisations to lead with distinction, says, "Part of the failure of our institutions to serve with distinction may be the interaction between two reinforcing elements: low levels of trusteeship and the concept of the single chief executive."[2] Indicating his further distaste for the single-leader system, he goes on to say, "To be a lone chief atop a pyramid is abnormal and corrupting."[3]

What Greenleaf has to say about institutions in general is particularly true of the church. Not only is the principle of the lone leader "abnormal and corrupting" but its impact on those who are the led can be astonishingly painful. Moreover, the failure to lead well results in the impoverishment of Christ's people. In such structures, the gifts of the many are not recognised and developed. The goal is not empowerment but submission.

Greenleaf is correct in his critique of the weaknesses of leadership in Western institutions. The abnormality of the "man at the top" syndrome, whether he is called CEO, or President, or Senior Pastor, is a cancer eating at the health of all human organisation. It is this cancer, extended through the expectations of younger leaders and reinforced by training institutions, that has created our present realities. The pervasiveness of this syndrome fulfils itself in Greenleaf's second target of responsibility, trustees, whether they come as synods or commissions, or elder boards. The man at the top syndrome has become our culture and as such does not allow for the creation of trustees of distinction. We are left to die the death of the strengths and weaknesses of the man at the top!

This is not an argument for an absence of leadership, or to suggest that no one should ever be accountable to a leader, but it is an argument against the kind of authoritarian leadership that can brook no questioning, that does not know how to team build and that fails to understand how humility and leadership belong together. Not only is the wrong kind of dominating leadership ineffective, it also violates the picture of leadership that we see in the New Testament.

Three passages of scripture paint the New Testament picture with regard to the leading of Christ's people. These passages lay a grid of expectation over all of the other necessary statements. They form the "culture" in which New Testament church leadership should operate. The first passage, Ephesians 4:11–12, deals with the object of leadership, its intended purpose. The second, 1 Corinthians 12, deals with the structure of leadership. (By structure we mean universal and foundational descriptions of leadership, rather than polity, which is open to historical and theological debate.) The third passage, Matthew 20, is where we receive an instructive description from Jesus regarding the very essence of leadership. Indeed, if any New Testament passage could be said to contain the essence of a theology of leadership in the New Testament, it would be this one.

1. The Purpose of New Testament Leadership (Ephesians 4:11–12)

While a great deal could be written on this passage, for our purposes it is sufficient to draw attention to two essential issues.

i. The missing element in leadership

We see in scripture that God often brings a structure into being which needs an element of completion in order to fulfil all that God originally intended. For example, in Genesis 1 and 2 we see how God created the world and then brought Adam into being with the intention that he might enjoy all that God had made. However, for this picture to be complete, God had to give Adam a companion, Eve, in order that God's original intention might be fulfilled.

We glimpse something of the same pattern in Ephesians. God has brought the church into being. The Holy Spirit is active in the life of the believers. The offices of elder and deacon give a basic structure to the life of the congregation, allowing for pastoral oversight and practical care. However, there is still something missing without which the people of God will not be able to fulfil God's purpose of equipping the saints, of building up the body of Christ. Ephesians 4:11 makes it clear that the missing element is that of the functions performed by apostles, prophets, evangelists, pastors and teachers.

The practical contribution of these ministry functions needs to come into the framework or structure of the life of the church to fulfil the purpose of the empowerment of God's people. Leadership that does not result in empowerment is severely lacking. Eddie Gibbs makes the point in his book *Church Next*, that growing churches are moving from bureaucratic hierarchy to apostolic networks. He understands that this has an implication in terms of flattening organisational structures,[4] but the introduction of the fivefold ministry gifts means much more than this in terms of the life of the local church.

Today, even in the difficult field of Europe, larger churches are emerging which we might call resource churches. Some use the term "Antioch churches", referring to the way in which the church at Antioch sent out leadership resources in a wider missionary enterprise. These larger "Antioch" churches almost always have all of the fivefold function present amongst their leadership. But not every local church will have all five of the functions mentioned in Ephesians in their midst. However, they do need access to those functions within a wider network. They also need to model the impact of team within their church if they are not to limit and even distort the shape of their local church.

Arguably all denominations started life in this way. In the early medieval period, larger churches often sent out preaching teams so that over time the minsters themselves extended their influence and often became the centre of a diocese. In the 19th century, large Baptist churches such as Spurgeon's church often became the sending centres for church planting movements which later consolidated as associations. The dynamism lay in the way that team ministry reproduced life in local churches. It was not individuals that were important but the impact of the mobilisation of the many.

My experience within the body of Christ over the last 33 years has led me to ask the question, "If any one of the functions of these gifted people is missing from the life of the church, what is missing?" As we shall see further on, what is missing is exactly what causes the church to miss its nature and purpose, and correspondingly lose its impact upon the world around it.

For a number of reasons, the church has tended to focus solely on the gifts of pastor and teacher and we have often located these gifts in the office called minister, priest or pastor. To make matters worse, that "office" has often been structured as the dominant leader in hierarchical terms. As Greenleaf observes we then die the death of the strength and weaknesses of the "man at the top"! That does not mean that the gifted pastor is not gifted by God, but apart from the other ministry gifts that single contribution is distorted.

This distortion has been around so long as to feel natural. But it is as unnatural as any of the worst heresies fought during the first few centuries. It is not necessary to document the precise history of this development but it is clear that the process was underway at a fairly early point in the life of the church. A number of creative missionary periods in the history of the church have interrupted this pattern, only for the dominance of a single clergy person to reassert itself later. In more recent decades, and especially as the non-Western church has superceded the church in the West, a new and widespread discontent with existing leadership patterns has emerged. That discontent has led to the development of a more biblically based diversity of the Ephesians 4:11 functions, as well as to a growing decentralisation of church forms and thus leadership practice.

My wife and I have travelled the globe serving national church leadership in over 50 nations of the world at some time in our lives. In Latin America, Africa and Asia, we have consistently found megachurches that have arisen in a variety of contexts. Megachurches have also arisen in the United States, but the differences between Western and non-Western expressions of megachurch are striking! For example, I have found few if any megachurches in America that have intentionally planted daughter churches. At best we have found a few among them who have planted a handful of other churches, and most of them were planted not because of a primary vision, but more because of the unfulfilled dreams of a group of people in the church, or a staff member.

The picture is very different in other parts of the world. I have rarely if ever found a megachurch in a non-Western context that was not systematically planting daughter churches. Most of them could point to hundreds of other churches that they had planted. They were not planting churches because it seemed like a good programmatic idea, but because down deep inside of them a different drumbeat was sounding. They did not exist to build a megachurch, but to extend the gospel into a people, nation, state, city or neighbourhood. They did not have to be taught to plant new churches: for them, planting new churches, by the releasing of new leaders, was like breathing.

For example, a church led by Pastor David Mohan, in Madras, India, has not only grown to be a church of more than 20,000 but they have also planted close to 200 other local churches and are still planting. It is very hard to find churches of significant size in the Western world that enjoy a similar planting record.

Why are the two pictures so dramatically different? One part of the answer is found in Ephesians 4:11. The average Western church is led by a pastor or a teacher, and thus, as created by God the Spirit, they focus on caring for truth and people. It is not that the church does not need the ministry of pastors and teacher but they must be part of a greater whole.

Left in isolation (which is what one-person leadership produces), the church they seek to lead dies the death of their strengths and weaknesses. But leadership in these other churches around the world, unencumbered as many of them are by the historical interpretation of this passage, plays out a different role.

In fact, leaders in such non-Western churches are not pastors or teachers in function, but apostles. This does not mean that such leaders do not also look like dominating individuals. To some extent, leadership in the church will always reflect something of the culture that surrounds the church – the role of the patriarch in south east Asia, the chief or tribal elder in Africa and the cult of machismo in some Latin American situations. However, despite their surrounding culture, many of these leaders have learned, sometimes instinctively, to cooperate with a diversity of gifted others in ways that most Westerners do not understand. The result is that they release much more of the energy provided by the Holy Spirit in and through Christ's people.

ii. Corporate impact

It is instructive that Paul does not describe the actual individual ministries of these gifted people. It is the corporate effect of their ministries that occupies his attention. They, all of them, were given by the resurrected Jesus to empower his people to do the work of ministry.

This idea of ministry must by design have encompassed the

two parts of the ministry that Paul has already described in Ephesians. On one side ministry is that which describes the life and witness of the individual. In chapter two he describes the sovereign work of God in creating us after the image of his Son, and giving to each and every one of us good deeds which he planned for us to do.

The actual context, culture or vocation in which each follower of Jesus is called to live and walk matters little. Every context, every culture and every vocation is a place where God has ordained his gospel story about Jesus to be lived and told. Every follower of Jesus is an equally important instrument of that story.

But there is another important view of the ministry. It is the cumulative effect of the whole body of believers, whether locally, city-wide, statewide, nationwide, or globally. It is this picture of the body that Jesus describes in John 17. Paul also described the importance of this impact in Ephesians 3:10 and 11. The individual stories of every Christian responding to grace and attempting to live out its implications, from Pentecost until Jesus comes, have an impact upon the unseen forces of eternity, and for all of eternity.

The measurable impact of those that we recognise as leaders should be to empower all of Christ's people to play out this eternal purpose on their personal stage of time, in whatever context, culture or vocation God leads them to. The degree to which any generation, or local manifestation of Christ's people, fails to grow in the incarnation of this reality reveals the failure of its leadership.

Nothing in the words of Paul should lead us to conjure in our minds the importance of any individual in leadership, or even to see any one of the functions as more important than any other. It is possible to claim that Jesus anticipated that these gifted people would actively cooperate and coordinate their impact in and on the body. Can the great burden that Paul confesses for and through the people of Christ, especially as seen in the letters to the Corinthians, leave us in any doubt that he was willing to be measured by the impact of the ministry of his team upon the body? Would Paul have been satisfied to sell books, teach seminars and produce videos if Christ's people had not measurably grown in their intimacy with the Heavenly Father, or in their incarnation of his gospel story about his Son, Jesus, to the world around them?

Is this not the precise picture of what we see in the book of Acts? As others have noted, it is appropriate to call this book the Acts of the Holy Spirit. For not only is the Spirit convincing, convicting and judging the world about its sin, he is equally working through gifted people to inspire and lead Christ's people to the full impact that God has designed in them and destined through them.

2. The Structure of Leadership (1 Corinthians 12:7–27)

The second passage, 1 Corinthians 12, presents a similar challenge to that of Ephesians 4:11–12. Here we need to focus on two salient concepts as they relate to leadership. The picture painted by Paul of the body is only a metaphor and so must be limited in its applications. But it is a metaphor that dominates the whole of the chapter, and as such must also be given credence. Paul's metaphor deals with foundational issues in relation to the leadership of the church.

Leadership must reflect the gifts given to the whole body. People in the leadership body are first and foremost followers of Jesus. They are not first of all leaders. Above all, they are Christians. All descriptions about the foundational nature of the church must also apply to them. Therefore they need to model what they teach. That can be something of a challenge to Christian leaders, living as they sometimes do in the rarefied atmosphere of the church. For example, leaders in evangelical churches frequently encourage church members to build relationships with those who are not Christians but do not always do so themselves. Leaders need to keep in mind the following principles in terms of the gifts of the Spirit.

Gifts are given to every one of Christ's people (verse 7). No follower is left without at least one Spirit-energised ability, and probably most if not all Christians have a mosaic of gifts. That almost certainly means that there are more potential leaders in the church than we sometimes imagine.

In making this claim, we need to remember that these gifts are not our personal possession. The individual does not possess them; they possess us, even as the Spirit lives in and through us to accomplish personal and earthly ends in the ministry of the gospel and ultimately in the sovereign completion of God's designs over human history. The Holy Spirit fully cooperates with my personality – we do not become robots – but he does so in ways that move his power through us for God's ends, not our personal fulfilment. Yes, the individual believer does feel fulfilled when he or she cooperates with such movement by the Spirit, but the giving is not primarily for personal fulfilment as if we were merely consumers of God's gifts.

The gifts exist for the common good (verse 7). If there was no common good that God saw fit to be accomplished through the gifts of individuals, orchestrated in and through the corporate body, then gifts would not be given. They are not for us to possess, adore or reject. They are for the common good of all and as such are intended to fulfil the purposes of God. The church was not given to us to act as a stage on which to perform our spiritual gifts. Rather the gifts are given to us for the benefit of the church.

The gifts that we receive are decided exclusively by the Spirit (verse 11). The individual does not decide which gifts he or she would like, nor have our Christian parents decided which ones they would like their children to have. The theological training school that we might attend cannot by such training guarantee that we will receive the gifts that our parents deem most important. The Spirit, without our consultation, has decided by his sovereign wisdom and for God's purposes the gifts we are to receive. Of course, God takes account of our personal history and our personality. He can be trusted to give us the gifts that will produce both our personal fulfillment, and God's purposes.

The place that those gifts play in the body are decided by God the Father (verses 12–26). No part of the body can deny the validity of another. No part of the body can think of itself as possessing the most important place in the configuration of the body. Indeed, we are left with this somewhat uncomfortable declaration by Paul that a healthy body does all that it can to both protect and honour the hidden and least publicly honourable parts of the body. A narrow understanding of leadership tends to focus on the more obvious gifts in relation to leadership. The consequence can be that we do not recognise the extent to which leadership of some kind is widely dispersed in the body of Christ.

So what are these principles telling us about the core structure of leadership? First, leadership of some kind is widely distributed amongst the body of Christ. Second, the task of the primary leaders of the church is to model and create a culture in which everyone naturally expects to find their gift and use it. Third, we change the shape of the church to respond to the gifts we find rather than try to force people into the structures we have regardless of gifting. Fourth, we recognise that mobilisation takes place most effectively when people are using the gifts that God has given them.

That sounds fine as a theory, but it takes a certain security in a leader to live with a structure like that. It is precisely when confidence in God is lacking that there is a tendency to fall back on position or office as the source for authority rather than recognising that true leadership represents the power of influence as compared with the power of position. Hopefully if we have understood the gifts of an individual well, the position that we give in a structure reflects the gifting (and so influence) of an individual appropriately, such that there is no dissonance between role and ministry gifting. On occasion, leaders don't always understand their own gifts and so fall back on the expectations of the people or their training. The consequence of this is that they then build team round the people they like, as compared with building a complementary leadership team which is harder to work.

But understanding the gifts and so the role of an individual is not an easy matter. Few people come with clear labels: as an apostle, a prophet, an evangelist, a pastor or a teacher. Most of those who are leaders come equipped with an edge that relates to one or more of those giftings, but there are a multitude of other factors that influence the way in which their particular ministry gift functions in the body of Christ. These other factors act as filters or lenses, which means that each of us makes a unique leadership contribution. Whatever the similarities might be, God never makes two leaders who turn out to be exactly the same. It is worth mentioning at least four of those filters.

First, the precise mix of giftings, not only in relation to the fivefold ministry functions in Ephesians but also in relation to other gifts will be shaded differently in every person. Second, the context or ministry situation in which these gifts will be used will vary and so influence the way in which those gifts are used. Third, the extent of the giftedness will impact the extent of the influence of a particular individual. Two people might be evangelists and effective when they preach but some seem to be called to a wider stage while others are used more locally. Fourth, personality plays a part in colouring the way in which gifts are used and ministries received.

The complexity produced even by these four filters, leaving aside the fact that maturity and growth will change and develop gifts and ministry, means that we need a setting of mutual grace and support in order for gifts to function well.

For Paul, God the Father, God the Son, and God the Holy Spirit represent a model of the kind of cooperation and coordination that is expected from the people of Christ. It takes the cooperative and coordinated ministry of all three to fully empower, engage and mobilise the body of Christ into its divinely ordained purpose. Whatever the role of the Father within the Trinity, no one could claim that he is somehow the "Senior Pastor" within the Trinity who demands accountability from the Son and Spirit. The words and attitude of Jesus himself are instructive in this regard: "Let your attitude to life be that of Christ Jesus himself. For he, who had always been God by nature, did not cling to his privileges as God's equal, but stripped himself of every advantage" (Philippians 2:5–7, Phillips). The Trinity, in its own mysterious way, is actively cooperating together in the full enabling of the body of Jesus to fulfil its role in the purposes of God.

God the Spirit is working various gifts into our lives. God the Son is working to place us into the right place at the right time within the worldwide ministry of the gospel through the church. And God the Father is working the area of influence of all of this, according to everything he understands about us. All of this the Trinity does without destroying who I am, or turning me into their mere robot. Yes, I am expected to submit to the perfecting work of the Holy Spirit and the word of God. The more I allow him to work the effects of the resurrection into my life, the more I will look qualitatively like the master, Jesus. And, by extension, the more effective will be the ministry of the gospel through my gifts and influence. Therefore one of the key roles of leaders is the identification of the internal yearnings that lie within the lives of the people in their church and subsequent equipping and releasing of this call.

The Trinity is performing something similar in and for the people of Jesus, when, in their coordinated and cooperative work, they fully enable each Christian for action. It is the great mystery of God that he has entrusted leadership to imperfect human beings. To one degree or another, our failure becomes his failure. But that is the greatness of God, and the strength of the model that he leaves us. He will not move people to do what in their hearts they have not decided to do. He is the master of working with human reality and maturation to fully accomplish his purpose.

Not only must leadership conform to the gift given by the Holy Spirit, but leadership must conform to the holistic nature of the body itself. The two most compelling reasons so far for a different kind of leadership than we have possessed in the West for so long is the model of the Trinity, and the holistic nature of the body. The context for discussion about leadership is of necessity within a discussion of the nature of the body of Christ. Take away the reality of the body, and we have no need to talk about leadership. Any leadership in the New Testament is by nature of, for and within the body of Christ. It must be defined by words and concepts that describe that reality. Any other discussion of leadership that takes it out of, or sees it in conflict with, the very way that God has created the body of Christ must be rejected.

All of this is why those in church leadership must be careful about applying marketplace principles to church leadership. When those principles conform to God's first truths, then they are applicable, not because they reveal a new truth, but because they conform to God's already given truth. When these principles cooperate more with the system of the day, no matter how utilitarian it is, they must be rejected.

The same principle applies to the teaching that we find on leadership in the Old Testament. There we can identify some very important and universal truths, relevant for all generations of leadership. But when the structure of the leadership in the Old Testament, and especially with regard to Israel, is brought into the church, it is wrongly applied. The church knows no kings, save for King Jesus. The church does not practise the priesthood of Aaron, but the priesthood of every believer. The temple is no longer found in a tent or a building, but the people of Christ themselves, both individually and corporately, are the temple in which and through which God dwells. In reality many churches have an Old Testament model of leadership in mind.

3. The Essence of Leadership

This leads us directly into the most important passage with regard to leadership within the body of Christ, Matthew 20:20–28.

The discussion between Jesus and his disciples is instructive because it shows so much about Jesus and his followers. First, we see the patience of Jesus. Imagine the reminder of human frailty that must have entered his mind with both the question asked and the response of the others later on. How long has he been modelling and teaching the opposite? Even though the eternal effects of the Fall on all men and women in Adam can and have been undone. There is still an impact on the way we think and act.

Second, we see the humanity of even the best of Jesus' followers. These individuals would go on to form the foundation for so much of what we know today about the eternal truths of God (Ephesians 2:19–21). But they too are shaped by a very human perspective. It is encouraging to see the change in their lives that occurs over the years recorded in the book of Acts and the other Epistles. That same account reveals the struggle that the followers of Jesus had in terms of living out community in the way of Jesus.

We can thank God for his gracious preservation of this very

human encounter. For in it we see three principles stated by Jesus that must dominate all other thinking about leadership. First, there is the acknowledgement that all of the other systems around them reflected their natural expectations. The Jewish religious system of the day and the Roman political system were oppressive top-down systems. They were an exact incarnation of the man-at-the-top thinking that comes so naturally to unredeemed men. It seems that Jesus was saying, "I know that this is the culture that surrounds you, and the flesh that possesses you."

All around us today there persists this same cultural reality, top-down, over-under. It is as natural as breathing for humanity. The same basic principle finds many cultural manifestations. It also dominates the religious landscape of the world we live in. By the second century after Jesus died, the most comfortable model of leadership found in man, the man at the top, was invading the church of Jesus.

It is highly instructive that Jesus does not begin his monologue with the disciples explaining how they might redeem such a model, because this model is unredeemable! This is the second principle that Jesus wants his disciples to learn; what he is about to say is not like anything they have ever experienced. Yes, we do live in a world filled with the cultural reality of such models of leadership. And, just like the residue of the flesh that remains in each of us until we meet him, it will impact the way we do business. But when we reflect upon the powerful words of scripture and the model of our Lord himself, we see that the ideal is something very "other" than what we have experienced or will fully experience in our lifetime.

This then is the third principle: "not so among you", the NIV says. With these few words Jesus rejects the leadership of man in favour of the enigma of God's own pattern of relating to his creation. Jesus himself is the incarnation of that model. All of the words of the Jesus model are antagonistic to what surrounds us, and is indeed in our hearts: servant, slave, not to be served, ransom! In spite of what seems to be overwhelming odds, the enemy without in the culture that surrounds us, and the enemy within in the flesh that remains, Jesus does not diminish the call to lead. He is not saying that leadership is there to fulfil people's whims, or to be a doormat to people's abuses. But he is making it clear that the man-at-the-top pyramid, found in the pastoral model crippling us today, is the opposite of his model. Even though Jesus rejects a strongly hierarchical model, he does not negate the important role of leadership. It is just that if they are to lead in his kingdom, it must be by his designs and standards.

How then can we understand leadership? First, leadership in the New Testament is probably best seen as a series of concentric circles rather than as a pyramid. The circles acknowledge the importance of leadership as foundational to the community of Jesus' people, and if viewed multi-dimensionally, also acknowledge that the life of the community is built upon the servant work of effective leadership. The circles also acknowledge the organic connection between those in the core leadership body, and the people in other leadership groups as well as the people of Christ in the church. Concentric circles of leadership, each relating to one another and pressing out into the rest of the body that has been given gifts and grace stories by the Holy Spirit, provide a better picture of the organic nature of the body as described by Paul in 1 Corinthians 12. It is a much more strategic way for leadership to empower the people for whom God has given them responsibility. True leadership is first and foremost relational and influential.

This is often a hard lesson for many in church leadership to learn. The visible church is a volunteer body and as such votes with its feet! If leadership is actively carrying out its mandate to empower these people to fullness and effectiveness, then relationship and influence are two of the most important tools that they have been given in this task. The closer that leadership can stay relationally to the people for whom they have responsibility from God, the more empowering will be their ministry. Many other issues do of course impact the ability of leaders to empower, but none more is important than relationship and influence. We see in Matthew 20 that Jesus had both!

Second, we have to remember that this passage paints the ideal. But we live in a real world and as such will always have to do battle with the culture that surrounds, and the flesh that is within. The decision to act within the Jesus model is a clear-eyed decision. The more often I reinforce it with the decisions that I make, the more likely that vision comes to an expression of reality. Once it becomes more visceral then I can begin to see my decision-making dominated, or at least heavily influenced, by a new way of thinking and feeling. The goal is to get to the place where I am acting in accord with the Jesus model without having to think about it.

This is the rub that we must live with. We will not always be able to act in this way. The reality within us that still needs to change will go on until we die. The culture around us is equally pervasive and inhibiting. The more egalitarian the culture, the more it may appear to cooperate with the Jesus model. Even the church operating in present-day North American culture (which is about as egalitarian a culture as one will find anywhere in the world) has still found a way to express the top-down system.

A glance at the church around the world reveals just about every conceivable variation of the system that Jesus rejects in Matthew 20. In combatting such a tendency, some principles are helpful. One, a commitment to make the empowerment of Christ's people one of our most important measurable milestones, something which will require the giving away of authority with responsibility. Two, a commitment to treat all leaders in concert with the principles in Matthew, Ephesians and 1 Corinthians, even when their cultural demands conflict with such principles. We may not be able to change the way that they act, but we can change what is in our own hearts. Three, to realise that the best that we may achieve in most cultures is a flattening of the cultural demand. The flatter the structure becomes, the closer it gets to the Jesus model.

The difficulty of not moving fully in concert with the model of leadership that Jesus reveals is that we limit the effectiveness of leadership to produce the kind of church that Jesus intended. That limitation adversely affects the church in terms of its power to impact the world in which we live.

In summary therefore, three principles are critical. First, leadership is always more than one. God never intended and scripture never teaches that the title "pastor" or "minister" or "priest" should be given to one individual who would then assume authority over others and work in isolation from them. There is no passage in the New Testament where leadership, in any dimension, is ever dealt with in singularity. Moreover, the organic nature of the body demands an organic leadership. The diversity of what the people of Jesus need in order to be empowered to all that God has for them naturally demands more giftedness than any one person possesses.

Two, the challenge of unity is diversity. So much of the contention within the body of Christ can be better understood as points of view seeded by the Trinity into the church, through our diversity of giftedness, for its protection, run amok! A simple spectrum chart reveals this predicament. If you write the gift of mercy at one end, and then describe for yourself some of the characteristics of that gift, then at the other end of the spectrum you note the gift of leading, and again note some of its characteristics, you have a picture of the problem. A strongly pastoral gift will view the world through the matrix of people, whereas some leaders who are driven to achieve a vision have a tendency to view the world through the matrix of tasks. If neither has learned to appreciate the diversity of gifts that the Spirit has given, and the point of view that each brings to the table, there will be conflict.

The same scenario can be played out for the gifted people listed in Ephesians 4:11. The diversity that the Trinity has seeded into the body of Christ, and into leadership, holds out either the great promise of full empowerment, or of bitter conflict. How we learn to deal with the importance of other gifts, in direct and necessary diversity to our own, will determine the degree of healthy relationships among people in leadership bodies, and ultimately the effectiveness of leadership.

Three, the outcome of leadership is always the same: Christ's people are empowered. They are empowered to practise their priesthood and live in intimacy with the heavenly Father. They are empowered to live the uniqueness of their personal grace testimonies in all of the relationships that God is bringing their way. They are empowered to use their Spirit gifts in all of those same relationships, as well as ministries that the Lord Jesus opens up for them. We could argue that this represents the minimum requirement of leadership and to that extent acts as a measure of whether someone is actually exercising effective leadership.

The power of the church is the Holy Spirit working in and through all of Christ's people by the empowering ministry of people called leaders, whom Christ has given to his people. These leaders, fulfilling cooperative and coordinated apostolic, prophetic, evangelistic, teaching and pastoral functions, lead Christ's people into: 1. greater intimacy with God the Father; 2. daily releasing of their grace testimonies; and 3. identification, training and releasing all of Christ's people's Spirit-given gifts into ministries. It is these ministries that will deliver the message of reconciliation to every person given to each local church to minister to.

NOTES

1.   James C Collins and Jerry I Porras, *Built to Last: Successful Habits of Visionary Companies*, Century, 1996, p. 171.

2. Robert Greenleaf, *Servant Leadership*, Paulist Press, 1977, p. 83.

3. Ibid., p. 63.

4. Eddie Gibbs and David Coffey, *Church Next: Quantum Changes in Christian Ministry*, IVP, 2001, p. 84.

CHAPTER EIGHT

LEADERSHIP TO CHANGE THE WORLD

In chapter one of this book we made the point that the church is growing around the world at an astonishing rate. The extent of the growth is such that there has probably never been a larger people movement in the whole history of the human race. Philip Jenkins, in his remarkable book *The Next Christendom,*[1] documents the extent of the growth in some detail. In doing so he makes the point that many Christians in the West, and particularly the leaders of the historic churches that would describe themselves as more liberal, from a theological and probably social perspective, seem either to be unaware of that growth or certainly unable to understand its significance.

This lack of awareness and understanding ensures that such leaders are unable to grasp the lessons that flow from this growth. It is almost as if they patronisingly assume that the growth will soon stop once the nations in which the church is growing become comfortably secularised like the West. Astonishingly, many even miss the lessons on their doorstep as huge churches emerge from amongst many of the immigrant populations in Western cities all across Europe, North America and Australasia.

Even more remarkable is the simple fact that this growth was entirely unexpected 40 years ago. At that time there existed a deep pessimism amongst Western missions about the future of world Christianity and especially about the future of Christianity in the very parts of the world where the church is now expanding at a rapid pace. In 1968 one demographic expert in the World Council of Churches made this prediction:

> Towards the end of this century Christians will comprise no more than eight per cent of the world's population – assuming that the present demographic growth will not be arrested in some unforeseen manner . . . Even the best missionary strategy with a conventional approach to the field of church planting and church growth will have no material effect upon this prognosis.[2]

We now have the benefit of living in the beginning of a new century and so we can use hindsight to discover what actually happened. According to David Barrett, the percentage of the world that claimed to be Christian in the year 2000 was closer to 33% than the predicted 8%. Why such a discrepancy? Was this just a case of poor expertise? Not entirely, because undoubtedly the demographic picture was not favourable for Christianity in the middle 1960s. But more importantly, the expert could hardly have been expected to predict that there would be huge people movements arising in parts of the world which were then thought to be somewhat unreceptive to the Christian faith.

In chapter eleven of this book, we explore in more detail the nature of movement and the ways in which movements develop, but for the moment we are concerned more specifically with the way in which leadership produces change and growth. In the previous chapter we looked at the development of a cultural environment in which leadership of a particular kind might flourish. We spoke of a different kind of leadership, one which seeks to work in teams and which reflects the

Ephesians 4:11 ministries. The goal of this kind of leadership is the empowerment of God's people.

Whenever we look at the dramatic growth of the church in previously unreceptive nations, we can locate unusual individuals, those of whom it might be said that they are exceptional leaders. We might expect these few, unusually gifted individuals to become leaders in almost whatever circumstances they find themselves. But it is the contention of this book that such leadership is potentially more widespread than we sometimes assume. We are suggesting that such leadership can be nurtured and encouraged just as it can be discouraged and lost.

The management expert, Peter Drucker, makes the following point: " . . . there may be 'born leaders', but there surely are too few to depend on them. Leadership must be learned and can be learned."[3]

To develop creative leaders, we need to understand the characteristics of that kind of leadership so that we may learn how to nourish the widespread emergence of leadership that can change the world.

The kind of leaders that can develop a culture of leadership development think differently and act differently. Max De Pree, a notable author on leadership, was surely right in claiming that leadership is more of an art than a science. There follows twelve descriptors of different thinking and different action that help to give a flavour of the art of leadership.

1. Seeing Differently

Bobby Gupta, an Indian pastor in Madras, was entertaining some friends from the West. They happened to be talking about some of the healings that had taken place in his church recently. One of the visitors from the West asked whether these events had been recorded in any way. Bobby was surprised at the question. "Why would we want to do that?" was his reaction. The visitor explained that Western Christians might well be interested in such unusual events. It soon became clear that this was a puzzle to an Indian evangelist who claimed that possibly 80% of those who became Christians in India did so as a result of the miraculous. He wanted to know what happened in the West.

Clearly there are many churches in the West that do see healings take place but Western Christians are interacting with a different worldview. One pastor in Birmingham, England, told me of a remarkable case where someone who was about to be operated on to remove a growth on their lung was prayed for. Just before the operation was due, a final X-ray was taken which showed that the growth had vanished. The consultant explained to the patient that in very rare cases there could be an instance of instantaneous remission. The patient responded that it could also be a miracle that had occurred through answered prayer. There was something of a clash of worldviews!

It is clear in talking to leaders in situations where the church is growing that most people see the world in terms of spiritual realities. For them, we do not live in a merely material universe. In talking to Christians from Asia, South America and Africa who are living in the West, it is clear that they bring a different way of seeing to their daily lives. They have an expectation that God is going to be active in and through them each and every day. That different way of seeing the world is foundational in terms of fostering leadership.

2. Living with Vision

It is obvious that leaders are people who talk about vision. But we need to be clear what we mean by vision. Max De Pree points out that very few people in the population have a gift for being visionary, but that leadership is not necessarily about being the author of vision so much as being a carrier of the vision.[4]

The casting of vision is a powerful activity and needs to be engaged in very sensitively. Some books on leadership speak of "BHAGS", by which is meant big hairy audacious goals. The difference between a BHAG and a regular goal is that the BHAG contains an audacious challenge that generates attention, engages the imagination and galvanises action on the part of those who are involved in making it happen. Kennedy's challenge to put a man on the moon within a specific timeframe was certainly a BHAG as compared with a goal like balancing the budget.

It is not the case that any BHAG will do as long as it is sufficiently audacious. Those who are casting vision need to be certain, not only that they have heard from the Spirit, but that they are talking to the right people. The challenge needs to be appropriate in relation to those who are being challenged. When it is appropriate then it will illicit a response whereby at least some people demonstrate initiative and begin to take responsibility.

Vision by its very nature is always located in the future. Those who are leaders will live in imaginative relationship with vision. They will see the future clearly; they will be able to articulate it. They can describe what it would look like and possibly even feel like when the future vision becomes present reality.

3. The Confidence of Conviction

In talking with leaders I am often struck by their confidence that something is going to happen. I spoke recently to a Brazilian pastor working in the New York and New Jersey area. He was responsible for church planting in his particular denomination for that region. It was impossible not to notice the quiet confidence he had that churches would be planted, that they would grow and that leaders would be recruited. That confidence relates to two areas. First, the conviction that God is able to do through leaders that which he has asked them to do. You may find some times of wavering. But when leaders close their eyes again at night, they will see and feel the compelling sense of vision once again. In a short time this rekindling of the vision will drive them back into action.

Second, good leaders have a deep-seated conviction about people. They are people who believe, sometimes against or in spite of the prevailing context, that people will follow if an appropriate lead is given. I do not refer to a dreamy idealisation that causes these people to ignore the difficulty of moving people towards a goal. Of course in younger leaders, their dreams may not have been tested by the realities that confront a leader when trying to implement a vision. But, for the mature person of vision, steeled by the lessons of life, there comes a conviction about people that is deeper than everyday encounters with people.

This does not mean that everyone will respond. But, in most cases, enough people will act enabling these leaders to lead people in accomplishing much more than many others ever believe that it is possible for people to do. Whatever the receptivity that the Spirit of God is producing in the midst of a given culture, leaders will take full advantage of it by moving God's human resources, the incarnated stories of his grace, into a purposeful harvest, far greater that than many others working in exactly the same context. They believe in the power of God through people.

4. Points of Access

Institutions which are in trouble are static in their self-understanding. The survival of the institution becomes more important than the reason for its creation. Ironically that perspective almost certainly ensures the death of the institution. Leaders who are consumed by a compelling vision care little for the institution – that is only a vehicle for the vision and can be reshaped. The goal for leaders who are creating movement is therefore to make the Christian message and its particular expression accessible. Everything that people need in order to come to faith, grow in faith, incarnate the faith, and extend the faith, must be accessible. By accessible we do not mean "user friendly".

Accessible means that people do not have to change their whole way of life to access the Christian message. Creative and determined leadership works out how to touch the lives of many people where they presently are. This is one of the fundamentals that makes cells or small groups so powerfully effective around the world. People do not have to go far to go. They do not have to go far geographically to access the friendship, community and accountability found in a cell. They do not have to go far culturally to see the gospel in their midst, lived out in marriages and families which have been transformed by its power. They do not have to go far linguistically to understand the message.

Good leaders innately understand the importance of making everything accessible. Even when you find them gathering thousands, or tens of thousands, of people into worship venues, you always find something more fundamental to their effectiveness behind the scenes. That fundamental lies in the fact that they are constantly imagining and creating accessible structures. Evangelism, training, discipleship and even multiplication are all founded on a principle of "take it to the people", rather than "bring the people to us". The formation of such flexible structures generates leaders at every level. Leadership is not raised to such impossibly high standards that few could ever hope to become a leader.

5. Releasing Responsibility

Dynamic leadership does not think first of how to retain control but of how to give away as much as possible. Leaders that produce movements are always looking for others to lead alongside them. The more developed the movement, the more you will see tens and hundreds of others leading with such founding leaders. Note that I say "with" and not "for". "For" is a uniquely Western idea caught most powerfully in the concept of staff. Staff means I help you do something. "With" means that both of us have found something greater and more important than both of us. The particular and often inherited structure that they are required to labour under does not stop these people from finding appropriate ways to release power, responsibility and people into leadership.

They understand, innately many times, but from scripture as they mature, that only people can truly fulfil the vision. Yes, money, opportunity and resources are needed. But, for these people, none of these are a supplement to the power of God working through his people to accomplish his ends. Followers sense this deep-seated belief and expectation, and they respond to it.

6. Finding a Way

Audacious challenges are rarely easy to accomplish. They are not impossible to achieve, but they are difficult. That is part of their audacity. If such challenges are not to fall by the wayside and become abandoned, there has to be a commitment to action. That does not mean a fully worked plan. The reality is that few audacious challenges have a clear pathway to fulfilment. The plan has to unfold over time. What matters therefore, in the first instance, is the creation of the kind of leadership that can live with the uncertainty of not knowing everything, but has a commitment to begin something, even if what is begun might prove to be a false start and have to be abandoned.

To some extent the confidence to live with a degree of uncertainty flows from a particular understanding of the nature of the body of Christ as seen in 1 Corinthians. That passage points to the need for mutual reliance within an organic team precisely because team needs to reflect a diversity of gifts. A full appreciation for the diversity of gifts given by the Spirit encourages leaders to believe that the organised elements necessary to fulfil the plan will come from someone else, if and when necessary.

Even though leaders are not always first and foremost experts in organisational delivery, it is often still the case that they will have developed some demographic awareness of their situation. I will often see detailed maps of where something has already been accomplished, i.e. where churches have been planted, and, where more churches could be planted. For leaders, these maps are always related to the full evangelisation of a city, or region, or even a nation. In other words, their vision is always extensive. Further, I am no longer surprised to see some form of written goals and objectives. I say some form, because each of these people will have organised themselves in ways that are consistent with their own culture.

7. Staying the Course

The kind of leaders we need will be persistent. I often discover that some leaders have run with a vision for decades and even when no progress is made for many years, they do not give up. Time, money, obstacles, even failure, are all ultimately irrelevant. Whereas most others would not even have started, they venture out. Where others would have ceased, they will continue to believe and act. Obviously, this could also be a weakness. But, in most cases, if the Spirit of God has been the originator of the vision, then persistence will be necessary.

Note that I add no definition of success. We are a generation conditioned to define success in less than biblical terms. These people, because they understand what God has asked them to do, and because it is related to his Kingdom, and its expansion, understand that fulfilling the vision and not just human terms of success must drive them. When God's people are growing in intimacy with him, we are approaching success. When God's people are fulfilling his designs for them, especially as it relates to the expansion of his kingdom, then we are approaching success.

8. Inspired by God's Previous Actions

Good leaders interact creatively with the missionary history of the church. There is something about men and women who have lived creatively in the past that catches the attention of these contemporary leaders. Creative leaders recognise the dilemmas that they face in the experiences of the past. Perhaps it is a pragmatism that weaves its way into their consciousness. Or possibly it is just an innate inquisitiveness that they are born with. Whatever the cause, there is in most good leaders a constant desire to read and study others who have passed this way before them.

There seems to be in such leaders an unconscious interplay between the dimensions of time, past, present and future, all interacting at the same time. The past lights up something in the mind, especially about how to accomplish the vision. That insight from the past however must be brought into the future and chewed on. The insights are compared to the present realities, squeezing from them principles or vicarious experiences that can be superimposed upon the future. It is this ongoing process, provoked by the vision, compared to others in the past, analysed in the present, that helps set the course for the future.

9. Generous Hearts

Good leaders give away more than is humanly reasonable. This, more than any other distinctive, may be what marks out the character, or different thinking, of creative leaders. The more they mature and the more they learn to bring the vision in line with the expansion of the kingdom of God, the more they will use any and all of their resources to see the kingdom grow.

New churches planted, thousands of people brought into the kingdom of light, are more important than the growth of their personal structure. They are most fulfilled when there is an explosion of the kingdom of God in their city and nation. Movements, not institutions and their survival, are what creative leaders are all about.

So, it is not extraordinary to find these people giving away what others set up structures to protect, if it can expand the kingdom. It is fair to say of them that they live with their hands open, always ready to give away.

10. Authenticity First

The heartbeat of good leaders is to see the life of the kingdom lived out with others with whom they are in relationship. Numbers, programmes, methods and size do not fire them nearly as much as the authentic Christian life. The joy of seeing grace lived out in communities where lives are being touched and changed motivates them to want to see authentic life multiplied. But they pay careful attention to quality before quantity.

Good leaders know that when the foundations of quality are right then growth and reproduction remain healthy. Large churches are never the goal, but healthy communities are. Paradoxically, the concern for quality produces the possibility of healthy numerical growth. On occasion, the leaders of large churches which are focussed on quality cannot always tell you how many people are in their churches. They are not counting heads; they are paying attention to the life that is taking place. Good leaders do not just do the right things; they know the value base that informs such action.

11. Burning the Rule Book

Good leaders understand the difference between ends and means. The end that is desired – the creation of healthy communities of believers, impacting the world around them – is sufficiently well understood that they can be very pragmatic about the means by which the end is achieved. Their values are written sufficiently deep that their pragmatic actions will not compromise the message but they know how to contextualise the delivery.

One church leader in a large denomination in Australia held the denominational handbook above his head while speaking to their annual governing body. He tore it in half and made the suggestion that he would be happy to throw one half of the rule book away to make life in their bureaucratic denomination somewhat simpler. And, he continued, it wouldn't really make much difference which half was thrown away. He was probably overstating his case but there is little doubt that most of our institutions are over-governed and under-led. The renewal of many structures can be aided by offering some "free fire" zones where creativity is given some free rein.

12. Start a Fire and Fan the Flames

Good leaders are not afraid to begin something. While many can be frozen by the fear of failure, good leaders are risk takers. That does not mean that they are irresponsible but it does mean that they recognise that you cannot always predicate the outcome of everything that you begin. They are aware that you cannot control the whole process from A to Z before launching something new. If we wait until we understand everything, it will probably be too late to take action.

The overall direction is more important than getting every detail in place. Of course, it is true that organisation and administration matter but it is important that organisation and the management of detail follow the vision; they can never drive the vision. To refer to Peter Drucker once more, effective leaders take action; they never simply talk about the action they might take.[5]

THE TEAM THAT DELIVERS THE VISION

If the twelve characteristics of good leadership that we discussed above create the leadership culture in which leadership might be learned or even caught, we also need to pay attention to the nature of the gifts that will be needed to produce such a culture. Bill Hybels, the Senior Minister of Willow Creek Community Church, makes the fascinating point that "the church demands a higher and more complex form of leadership than business does".[6] Creating the team structures that deliver a higher and more complex form of leadership requires careful consideration.

In the previous chapter we described the importance of bringing all five of the ministry gifts listed in Ephesians 4:11 into the leadership mix. We noted that not every church will be able to locate all five functions in their leadership team but that local congregations should at least have access to such a gift mix in the network of relationships that the church engenders over time. But even when all five functions are present, those functions alone will not be enough to be build a leadership team that can deliver a vision.

A mix of four key skills must either be in the leadership team or the leadership team must have access to these skills. First, the gift of leading itself. Here we are using the term "leading" in a very specific sense. It is used to describe the management of the future. Those who have apostolic, or prophetic, gifts will be those whose attention is fixed on tomorrow. They will not allow the team to lose sight of the purpose towards which the church should be headed. Their fixation with tomorrow might be sufficiently great that they are unable to connect tomorrow with today but nevertheless their passion for the future is vital in keeping a healthy focus in place. They need to exercise personal discipline to ensure a connectedness between tomorrow and today.

Second, the gift of managing people. This gift focusses on how today is managed in the light of tomorrow. Often this gift is located amongst those who have a strong pastoral gift but it should not be seen as entirely synonymous with the ministry gift of pastor. On occasion, some pastors are so driven by an empathy for people that while they can express love and compassion, they are not able to manage people in a team setting. The management of people can be seen in the creation of team harmony. People are managed well when their gifts are understood and used well in the team. Pastors, no less than apostles, need to work on the equipping of God's people.

Third, the gift of organisation or the management of structure. The management of people is not the same thing as building the organisation that can deliver the programmes that will be required to implement the vision. Effective organisations contain people who understand the difference between strategies and tactics. They may be inspired by a vision of the future but their focus is firmly on today and the kind of structures that will be required to make an idea happen on the ground.

Fourth, the management of detail or administration. This gift is not always located in the primary leadership team and is sometimes seen as a deaconal or serving function. However, if the management of detail is not located within the primary team, it must not be far away if delivery is to take place. The translation of ideas into the when, who, where and how of practical administration is part of the necessary accountability structure without which the greatest dream will never transpire.

The bringing together of this kind of gift mix should result in a happy team. Happy teams have fun together and that is part of the story. Grasping a big, hairy, audacious goal and seeing it come into being is sufficiently energising that those who are part of that kind of team need no prompting to get up in the morning. The creation of that kind of team allows us to grasp the mission and put it into practice.

NOTES

1. Philip Jenkins, *The Next Christendom*, OUP, 2002.
2. Cited in Martin Robinson, *Winning Hearts, Changing Minds*, Monarch, 2001, p. 80f.
3. Peter Drucker, "Your Leadership is Unique", *Leadership: A Practical Journal for Church Leaders*, Fall, 1996, p. 54.
4. Max De Pree, "How to Create a Lively and Harmonious Future", *Leadership: A Practical Journal for Church Leaders*, Summer 1994, pp. 18.
5. Drucker, "Your Leadership is Unique", p. 55.
6. Bill Hybels, "Up to the Challenge", *Leadership: A Practical Journal for Church Leaders*, Fall, 1996, p. 56.

CHAPTER NINE

LEADERSHIP AND THE DISCIPLINE OF MULTIPLICATION

In the previous chapter we noted that some of the most dramatic expansion of the church has taken place over the last 40 years in areas that were previously considered to be unreceptive to the gospel. The two most obvious examples are Latin America and China. Missionaries to both those parts of the world up until the 1970s had either struggled to make converts, despaired of discipling converts, or, as in the case of China, been forbidden by the state to operate at all.

What was it therefore that changed the spiritual climate? It is obvious that in China, the end of persecution during the Cultural Revolution and the emergence of a more open attitude to the church helped. But that does not explain the rapid development of a people movement. It is also clear that in Latin America, the complex political situation, combined with a realignment of the Roman Catholic church alongside the poor, produced uncertainty and a degree of tension which caused some to look for spiritual answers elsewhere. But even these changes do not explain the dramatic shift in receptivity to the gospel that has taken place in nation after nation during the last 30 to 40 years.

I do not want to propose a single, simplistic explanation but it does seem to me that we gain a sense of what took place in the title of one of Peter Wagner's books, *Look Out, the Pentecostals are Coming*. This somewhat alarming title (the title was changed in subsequent reprints) points to some fascinating personal transactions that took place in patterns that led to a multiplication of witness. Let me illustrate the point from a single conversation.

Recently I was in conversation with a Brazilian minister whose father had been the founder of a new denomination that began in Brazil in the 1960s and was part of the dramatic growth of the Protestant community in that land. His father had been a minister in a mainstream American Protestant mission in that land for many years. In common with other ministers and missionaries, he had found the population to be somewhat unreceptive to the gospel. But all that was due to change. In the early 1960s he became ill with cancer and the diagnosis was not hopeful. He was likely to die. He then experienced a remarkable healing. The cancer completely disappeared after he was prayed for. It was what we in the West might call another case of instantaneous remission.

Naturally he told his brother ministers of this remarkable healing, but his news was not greeted with unbridled joy. He was informed that his denomination did not believe in healing and he would need to recant his testimony. As you might imagine, a man who had newly received his life back was not inclined to do that and he insisted that he had indeed been healed. His refusal to withdraw his testimony led to his expulsion from the denomination. He then founded his own new denomination, which possibly unsurprisingly grew dramatically as news of his testimony spread.

Recently, a British minister told me of someone for whom he had prayed for healing. She had been brought to a meeting by her husband who was not a Christian. During a particular conversation, the unbelieving husband discovered that he had been healed of a complaint he had had for many years, and he began to tell his neighbours of what had taken place. Soon, some of his neighbours were turning up at church.

I want to suggest that when the people of God begin to speak about the acts of God then receptivity to the gospel rises. Might it just be possible that in unreceptive lands, the people of God either don't see the hand of God at work (seeing instead only instantaneous remissions), or even when they do see the actions of God, they fail to speak to others about them, fearing either rejection or mockery? My suspicion is that what has happened in Latin America and China is that there has come a multiplication of such testimony which has resulted in a significant rise in receptivity to the gospel within relatively short time periods.

It is obvious then that we should be encouraging the people of God to speak about the actions of God in ways that allow a significant multiplication of witness to take place. How then might it be possible to work to create structures in which multiplication of witness and growth take place?

The most obvious structure in which multiplication of witness can occur is through the encouragement of church planting, but that represents only one vehicle. The principle of multiplication needs to be embedded in all that we do, whether church planting or through cell groups, or in evangelistic processes such as Alpha, or through the renewal of existing structures. This chapter looks at the undergirding principles that allow such multiplication to operate.

1. The Church of Jesus Christ is Intended by God to Multiply and Grow

It is one thing to believe that in some theoretical sense the church is intended to grow. It is another to believe that in some way that principle involves us. Once we are gripped by a conviction that we are somehow involved then we are making a decision. That decision implies that because such a principle is true and it involves us, we need to find a way to enable that growth to happen. Whether by church planting or by expanding existing structures, leaders need to come to the place where they are determined to find a way to multiply and grow the church of Jesus Christ.

The availability of resources, training or obvious opportunity become secondary considerations compared with the conviction that somehow the church must grow. The leaders of growing churches around the world, regardless of ability, have arrived at that conviction. The methods are as varied as the people involved, even if the trained eye can detect familiar patterns that underlie those methods.

2. Whatever God is Going to do in the World, He is Going to do Through ALL of Christ's People

No other entity on earth contains such an astonishing diversity as that which is found in the body of Christ. Its full release reveals the complete story of God's grace which is then released into every conceivable human context.

3. Whatever God is Going to do in the World through Christ's People, He is Going to do Primarily Through a Decentralised Structure

Many of these leaders may not be able to verbalise this conviction, but they certainly live it. The power of God's people, released into every conceivable relationship that Christians have: in their families, in their neighbourhoods, and in their marketplaces, is galvanised by these leaders for action. No matter how large their particular church, they are always more concerned about those who have not yet been reached.

4. All Multiplication Processes Begin with Prayer

It is not just any prayer that matters. There is a qualitative dimension that makes the prayer of determined leaders effective. Their praying is visionary. By this I mean, they not only ask God where and how he would want them to work, but they expect him to answer. In prayer they expect from God, but also anticipate what God is going to do long before he actually does it, through their obedience.

Their praying is targeted. They have places in mind that need the testimony of the gospel. They do not have to be convinced that they and the church are God's tools, therefore prayer focusses on the village or neighbourhood where they believe God wants them to be obedient and expand their witness. All kinds of ways are found to practise this reality: prayer walks, door-to-door visits asking for specific things to pray for, and so on. But always, they are targeting their expectations from God in prayer.

Their prayer is expectant. God, through their obedience, will bring people to himself. God will grow the church of Jesus in that place, and in every place where there presently is no gospel witness. He will provide the money, leadership, and the opportunities.

I want you to notice that this kind of praying produces some very important effects. It focusses attention on mission and away from maintenance. It is all too easy for church life to become focussed on new buildings, new furniture, better lighting, better programmes and improved materials. There is nothing essentially wrong with such improvements except when they become the sole focus of our energy as compared with a mission focus which lies beyond the life of the church. A mission focus looks first at those who are outside the church before it ever looks at the internal needs of the church.

Further, this kind of praying produces an emphasis on obeying God in everyday lives and witness. By this people are helped to understand a fundamental reality of the Christian life, of moving from the kingdom of darkness to the kingdom of light. Our lives are the primary conduit that God uses to tell his story of grace to the world! Status is unimportant. God is able to move through any and all of his children, and what they do for a living becomes a context in which he will do it. All of this is the natural way in which God has ordained that his children should live. Personal growth, the growth of marriages, families and Christian relationships, played out before a watching world in the marketplace and the neighbourhoods where we live represent that raw material that God uses to show himself to the world. This becomes the reason for living rather than the accumulation of fame, fortune or wealth.

That kind of praying sets its eyes on eternity. Paul says to Timothy in his first letter to him that he is to teach the wealthy not to be arrogant nor to put their trust in earthly wealth. Instead they are to live with their hands open and invest in the true bank in heaven. In this day of consummate personal gratification, we have an urgent need to learn that time is defined by eternity, not vice versa.

This kind of thinking makes available all of the resources that God needs in order to do his work of grace telling to the world. This kind of praying brings the power of God to bear on the lives and context of ordinary believers! Given such conviction and obedience, what should we expect to happen? Exactly what does happen. People are won to Christ and churches multiply!

5. Multiplication is Based upon Good Research

Research focusses prayer! It presents believers with real people with real needs to pray for. Putting a face to the target through research gives God the Holy Spirit the opportunity to bring those people and their needs to our consciousness on a regular basis. We discover that there are more foreigners in our midst than we had known. We are startled to discover more single mothers or university students or hearing impaired than we had thought. The real needs and situations of our neighbours come powerfully to our eyes, and we are compelled to ask, what would God have us do?

Not only does God act as we pray, but we act in concert with him. There is something very powerful about seeing the faces of real people and pursuing the visions and goals that God has given to us. People by the tens, as they realise the needs around them, hear the good news on a regular basis that they are the fullness of God's provision. They begin to hear the prompting of the Holy Spirit on their own. It is a common experience for such churches to be filled with people who have been given a "mini-vision" by the Holy Spirit for some piece of the demographic and ethnological mosaic surrounding their church community. Leaders in such churches present the "need" as it is discovered through research, trust God to act in his people, affirm their callings and empower them to act.

Research has a direct bearing upon pre-evangelistic ministry. One of the weaknesses of modern-day evangelism is that it fails to draw the basic lesson of the parable of the seed and the sower. Every good farmer knows that if you don't plant any seed, you won't have a harvest. The farmer also knows that the harvest is not to be expected the day after the seed is planted. It takes time for the seed to germinate and grow. Water, sun and weeding cooperate together to prepare and anticipate the harvest. So it is with evangelism. Seed must be planted, and planted widely. That seed must be planted with no immediate expectation of harvest. But, along the way, the church must continue to water and weed, while the Spirit of God provides the unseen force. Then, and only then, will there be true harvest.

Good research provides a great opportunity for the multiplying church to work in this way. Door-to-door contact, focussed prayer, community events, evangelistic events, and the building of a network of personal relationships all cooperate to tell us something very important about the area to be reached. Those activities act to prepare the field for the serious work of proclaiming the gospel by the most appropriate means.

Finally, research is mandatory if we are to build the correct Spirit-energised evangelistic strategies that will bring in the harvest and grow the church. Every good fisherman understands this principle. One kind of bait works for one kind of fish, while another very different bait works for another fish. So it is with evangelism. The journey of every person in the world is known and understood by the Spirit of God. He has given to us the privilege of working with him in this evangelistic ministry. But we are not all-knowing as he is. We must find other ways to determine what people are thinking, what questions they are asking, and what particular aspect of the provision of God to begin with as we present the gospel.

Unless good and thorough research is undertaken, we cannot expect to harvest all that God the Spirit is preparing in the hearts of the people in our community. This is the primary reason you can see two different Christian groups working in the same context, and with the same people, but with vastly different results. One, whether innately or through good research, understands the people they are attempting to reach. The other assumes that they know what they are doing, even without a good idea of the people they are committed to reaching. One is proactive in touching people where they are, and as they are. The other expects all people to respond equally to any effort, no matter how culturally insensitive their actions might be. Good research is the precursor to good strategy.

6. Multiplication Demands a Proactive, Consistent and Broadly Spread Ministry of Evangelism

Methods to do evangelism abound, and who can say what will work until it is actually tried? Since the needs of people are diverse, so too are the ways in which they will be reached with the gospel. Effective evangelism will be diverse in its methodology, cyclical in its application and ongoing in terms of giving people repeated and personal opportunities to decide for or against the gospel of Jesus.

I saw this powerfully demonstrated in one colleague's church planting training and actions. First, their evangelism is research based. Once they have discovered where people are and what they think, they move in a multiplicity of ways to access those people with the gospel. In the first several months, the church planting team is expected to make at least 350 contacts with the gospel. They are so committed to this, that no further training can be received unless this is done.

Second, all evangelism is focussed on the incorporation of converts into the body of Christ. They are not doing evangelism to simply win people to Christ. They are sowing the seed of the gospel, harvesting those whom the Spirit is calling, and incorporating them into the body of Christ in that place. Where there is little or no incorporation into the grace life and gospel ministry of the church, one must wonder if biblical evangelism has resulted.

We are in need of a fresh look at the content of the gospel story that we are sharing with people. Emphasis upon new life in Christ, freedom from sin, or eternity in heaven, is incomplete and inadequate. It is incomplete because this is not where God begins the story of the salvation that he is offering to humankind. Since creation, God has been working to restore humankind to his God-created purposes: fellowship with him and representation of his being, character and designs here on earth.

It is inadequate because any telling of the gospel that does not begin with this biblical content has a difficult time naturally producing the kind of discipleship described by Jesus: a style of discipleship not only demanded in the New Testament, but the one upon which all of the expectations of the full mobilisation of Christ's people is based.

Anything less than this falls short of the grace that God has worked through Christ, into his children, and through them into the world. It is this grace, its story and living in the human flesh of every redeemed child of God that is the fulcrum of the life of faith and church. These kinds of churches make what so many deem extraordinary, simple ordinariness! Since the foundation of the world God has been in the business of making apparently ordinary people the instruments of his extraordinary message and ministry!

Third, as was mentioned above, the story of the gospel must be given in a repeated fashion. They are not dropping gospel bombs on people. Nor do they expect people to make decisions totally outside of their network of relationships. People in the community that is being worked with need time to hear, see, feel and relate to the gospel. They need to hear the true call of scripture, namely that God is calling them to be reconciled to him!

It is here where so many of the present forms of evangelism fail contemporary people. We are in pragmatic conflict over the point versus process nature of salvation, while to the infinite and all-knowing God of the heavens, the point is fully known; I am finite and limited in my knowing. It is far better for me to embrace the process that people go through in coming to saving faith, and cooperate with it!

It is essential that we create an environment where people regularly and repeatedly see a demonstration of the story of grace. First, because our mandate is not to save people. God does that. As people are drawn into the orbit of the message of grace lived and told by the church, God will draw them into believing. Then he will add to the church those who are being saved. Our objective cannot be to "grow" the church, but to live and give the grace found in the gospel in such a way that the environment is created for God to do what only he can do.

Second, because it is our responsibility to provide the opportunity for people to fully hear and understand the story. It is the life of the community of faith that provides the context in which people have the opportunity to make their decision for or against Jesus. This hearing and understanding will take interaction, dialogue and community contact for most people to come to faith. Such a process cannot be simply based upon the programmatic declaration of the gospel, but must be connected to the relationships and life of the people of the church.

Third, their approach to evangelism is extremely pragmatic. If it works, they continue using it. If it does not work, they discard or adapt it. They have learned early on that the message is inspired, but the mode of transmission is not. Since they are compelled by God to fulfil his loving mandate, they are equally compelled to continually assess how they do it.

7. Good Multiplication Processes Organise People into some Pattern of Small Groups as Soon as Possible

The term "small groups" in this context is a generic description of a highly effective function that is universally required. Whatever we call them, people need to be organised into groups of ten to twelve for personal interaction, and for the powerful living and declaration of the gospel. Of the many positive things that could be said about small groups, four elements are important.

i. These groups represent the initial stages of harvesting

These forums are the natural place to gather new believers and people positively predisposed to keep hearing the gospel. They are safe havens for people to open themselves and their needs to people who care, who pray and who will take action. They are the safest and sanest place for interested people to continue asking questions about the gospel. They are the clearest place to see the gospel dressed in the lives of real people living out the distinctive relationships that God is giving to them.

ii. *These groups are the best forum for* discipleship

This is the place where people can unmask some of their deepest needs. It is also the place where the ministry of the word and the Spirit can be directed at meeting those needs. It is the best place to find out how people are doing in the Bible's most important thresholds. Are we growing in intimacy with God? Are we living out the distinctiveness of our personal grace testimony and experience? Are we discovering and using our gifts?

iii. *These groups are the best place to keep all of Christ's people focussed upon* sharing the good news *into all of their relationships*

As uncomfortable as it may be, these intimate meetings are the best place for each of us to be asked for names of people whom God has placed on our hearts. Then as the group prays together each week, for these people to see, and report back, how God the Spirit wonderfully provides opportunity for us to bear witness. Of all of the things that believers do, this is the most powerful, to bear daily witness through both word and deed to the transforming power of the gospel of Jesus.

iv. *These groups are the best place to initiate* leadership development

It is ground level zero as it were. As new leaders are identified and begin their journey of responsibility, this is the best venue to grow them in the purpose, vision and values of the church body. It is the best place to see how to mobilise people. It is the best place to measure the gifts and roles of every burgeoning leader. It is the first place that every new leader ought to start their growth in the responsibilities of leadership. It is the place where the existing leadership should spend the majority of its time and energy in training.

8. Multiplication Requires that we must Begin Almost Immediately to Spread the Load of Responsibility by Training New Leaders

It is an inviolable rule: you can expand and extend the gospel only as far as you prepare others to take the responsibility with you. The place of the greatest emphasis needs to be the local church. Few would now argue that Christ gave gifted people to the church. He gave them apostles, prophets, evangelists, pastors and teachers, to empower others to do the work of the ministry. Their effectiveness is measured more by what others do in obedience, than by their own particular activities. Their effectiveness will be seen by history to be directly related to the time they spent preparing others in and for leadership in the local church and its gospel ministry.

i. Training leaders is the first step toward the full mobilisation of the church

I had always assumed that preaching was the primary way to mobilise people. I no longer believe that. I still believe in the importance of preaching and teaching, but not out of relationship to the importance of other actions as well. If I were to start over again, I would spend at least 50% of my time in training and preparing other leaders.

There is something about the relational transmission of purpose, vision, values and life that happens one-on-one, or in small groups that does not happen in communicating biblical truth to congregations. The latter is necessary to assist in motivating people to practise their own priesthood. But the former is mandatory to spread the load of responsibility, unite the many gifts necessary to perform the leadership function, personally to touch more of the believers, and thus, to see them actually empowered, not simply motivated, to action.

ii. Training leaders is the first step towards multiplying the church into cells, congregations and new churches

It seems to go without saying that in order to multiply anything, more leaders are needed. So it is with effective people that I have met from all over the world. They extend the church, and thus the gospel, far beyond others of their generation, not because they are smarter but because they raise up so many others to join them!

They do this by creating immediate opportunities for new and potential leaders to take responsibility within the life of the church. By "life of the church", I do not mean that new leadership serves only to keep the programme of the church going. It goes without saying that all churches need a certain number of leaders and people working to maintain the necessary programmes of a church. But the success of a church, as we have tried to define it in the previous pages, is measured more by how many people and how much leadership a church is able to release into opportunities outside of the ongoing maintenance of church life.

Churches that are creating multiple forms of evangelism, organising people into small groups and planting new churches, always have new places to put new and potential leadership. Moreover, these opportunities are not only the place of service but they are the point of training as well. It is good to have interactive and formalised training in local churches. Such training in the purpose, vision and values of the church, as well as training in personal spiritual disciplines and skills, is mandatory. But it should be obvious that doing is the best venue for real training.

iii. Training leaders is the primary task of the core leadership of the church

At one level, leadership is a word to describe a function. That function is best carried out by a diverse group of people united around a vision that God has given to them, and founded on firm convictions about the mission of the church in the world. Only this kind of leadership can truly train others of like kind. We can thank God for the training that goes on in and through organisations outside local churches. But that training only serves to supplement what must be going on as a part of the life of local churches. Growing movements understand and practise this!

9. Multiplication Structures are Organised around Purpose, Vision and Values

This is a point that has less significance in some places in comparison with others. In nations coming out of despotic forms of government, finding legal status that can sometimes mean freedom to survive is of great importance. Where freedom is assumed, this need may be felt less urgently.

But the need to structure the church in such a way as to maximise the purpose, vision and values, is imperative. Moreover, that structure needs to provide for a yearly review, and plan building processes in whatever way is consistent with the particular culture. As I listen to those who are multiplying the church, I am reminded that this need has great diversity, but also some great similarities.

The diversity of how churches structure and organise themselves will be dependent upon many factors. It will depend upon the particular denominational affiliation of that church. It will be shaped partly by the doctrinal convictions of the leadership team. And, it will be influenced by the culture and history of the nation in which it is situated.

But there are some important similarities that such organisational/structural demands share.

i. The point of organisation is an important juncture in the life of the new body when multiple congregations can be anticipated

I think of another colleague who pastors a large, growing,

cell-based, church planting church. In nine short years they have grown a church of over 2,000 people, planted over 250 others, and developed just about every evangelistic strategy one could think of. There are many reasons that this body has grown, but none more important than that they have structured themselves to be friendly to growth and the opportunities that growth brings.

Though they meet in three services in the centre of town on Sundays, they meet in multiples of congregations throughout the week, and hundreds of cells all over the city. The way they design their structure facilitates this life!

ii. How one structures and organises the church gives birth to the opportunity to nurture life in its people, and thus leads to multiplication

The average Western church is organised to survive. A few are organised to become large. But I know of few churches in the Western world that are organised to nurture life in such a way that they multiply. This is the beauty of the small group structure. It can work more closely with and in people to see the fruit of the Spirit and the life of Jesus growing in them. It can work more closely to assist people in living and telling their grace testimony. It can work more closely in identifying and releasing new leadership. And it can work more effectively in releasing vision in a majority of people.

Such a structure is not just an add-on to an already overburdened programmatic church. It is the very life of its existence. Nothing that threatens it is allowed to live in its midst. Everything must yield to the priority of mobilisation and multiplication!

10. Every Church Must be Impregnated with a Vision to Multiply Itself and Its Internal Structures

Given the human tendency to self-preoccupation and self-preservation, this is something that must be constantly worked at. If it is not implanted into the very DNA of the church at the beginning, it will be hard to protect and much harder to effect.

One can see this clearly demonstrated in the words and life of all movements. In these movements, churches do not see themselves as an end in themselves. They believe and practise almost without struggle the quest to multiply. It should be possible for every church in the world to plant at least three other churches in their lifetime. By lifetime, I mean a span of ten to fifteen years. It is at least a place to begin.

In order to begin, the cycle of churches that exist only for themselves must be broken. Breaking this cycle where it already exists, though necessary, is admittedly much more difficult than planting new churches that think no other way. It is almost always true: you get what you plant!

Is it possible to encourage churches to take the principles of multiplication to their heart? It has certainly proved to be so in the many parts of the world where the church is growing. It is always easier to accomplish where receptivity to the gospel is high. Receptivity undoubtedly rises when the people of God repeatedly talk to others about the actions of God.

CHAPTER TEN

DEVELOPING MISSIONAL STRATEGIES

On occasion, the missionary nature of the faith has been expressed in spontaneous and unplanned forms. But even in the apparently spontaneous context of early Christianity, writers such as F F Bruce detect a strategic intent in Paul's evangelistic thrust. In his book *The Spreading Flame*, he notes:

> A Roman colony was a community of Roman citizens planted at a strategic point of communications, to safeguard the interests of Rome in that outpost of empire. Paul's missionary eye picked out these strategic outposts and envisaged them as strategic centres in the spiritual kingdom which he was proclaiming and extending. Roman colonies played an important part in his successive plans of campaign.[1]

The Celtic saints were said to have taken to their coracles and then to have allowed the wind and the waves to take them to wherever God intended them to land. However, even then, Celtic saints had a strategic intent behind their wanderings. The intention was always to establish a community and from there to take the gospel message to the surrounding hinterland. St Aidan, having established a community on Holy Isle, began preaching missions to the most remote communities within the kingdom of Northumbria. The desire was to reach all people with the gospel.

The impetus to reach all people, not merely to maintain the structures, is very strong in a missionary faith. Whenever the church has been renewed, strategies to reach everyone in the population begin to arise. The early medieval period in Western Europe saw the rise of the minster model. The minsters were preaching centres and to a large extent the various parishes grew up around those preaching centres as a mechanism for reaching all. The Methodist circuit and the Baptist district were both originally mission models to allow a strong sending church to influence a wider area and so reach more people with the gospel. The late 19th century saw the rise of city missions, some of which appointed evangelists on a street by street basis. The plan was to ensure that every person had an opportunity to hear the gospel on a regular and systematic basis.

The collapse of a missionary heart in the church sees a corresponding diminution in intentional strategies for reaching all people in a given area. In other words, churches hope they will grow but fail to take responsibility for taking the gospel to those beyond the church. There is almost the feeling that it is the responsibility of the church to preach the gospel but it is the responsibility of those outside the church to come and hear it. Once again, in a previous paradigm, when most people accepted the truth of the Christian faith and saw clearly the social usefulness of the church, the notion of people coming to the church to hear the gospel was a very acceptable strategy. That strategy was strengthened by the idea that every community should have a church.

The late 19th century in Britain and the greater part of the 20th century in North America saw a huge rise in the number of congregations. The growth in church extension was part of an attempt to ensure that a church was available within walking distance (and later driving distance) of every person, particularly in the new cities and towns. Programmes designed to offer multiple contacts with individuals in the communities surrounding church buildings then reinforced the widespread distribution of churches.

Those programmes could be as diverse as Sunday School, men's groups, women's groups, youth groups, senior citizens' groups, choirs, educational classes, walking clubs, cookery classes – almost anything that met a need and which provided opportunities to build relationships and multiple connections with a local church. At the high point of such church life (1910 in the United Kingdom and possibly the late 1950s in North America) a very high percentage of people were affiliated to one church or another even if they were not actually recorded as members.

As we noted in chapter six, we are currently living between the collapse of an earlier paradigm (one minister, in one building, in one parish) and the emergence of a new paradigm. Most of us are very aware that the large number of people in the communities that surround our churches no longer come to the programmes that churches put on. The virtual disappearance of children from Sunday School in the United Kingdom, since 1945, is just one illustration of the collapse of programmes as a key element in the life of the church.

It is not that there is anything wrong with programmes as such; it is simply that the underlying motivation for people attending Christian programmes, namely that it was important to connect with a church, is no longer present. People are still attending all kinds of programmes but they are now to be found in colleges of further education, in gyms, in yoga classes and in a multitude of other activities both formal and informal. Programmes can still be effective for churches but the basis on which programmes are offered would need to be different.

To some extent, a concentration on programme can flow

from confusion about means and ends. Programmes can all too easily become ends in themselves rather than a means to exercising the true purpose of ministry. All too often, attention focusses on the success of the programme with less attention devoted to its missional impact.

What people do with their priesthood, in terms of nurturing intimacy with God as a regular pattern of life, should be non-negotiable. If God has worked his grace in each one of Christ's people in a unique way, then what they do with their grace testimony in all of their relationships is indispensable. If the Holy Spirit has given gifts to every person in the body of Christ to use in life and ministry, then discovering and using them is imperative. If the body of Christ is God's chosen incarnation into the world for this time and place, then how people live their interpersonal relationships among each other cannot be relegated to secondary consideration.

The consequence of concentrating on programme as compared with the empowering of people is that the local church tends to think of itself as the reason, focus and end of ministry. In truth, the church is not the object of ministry, but is instead the instrument of the ministry into the world, which is the true object of ministry of the church. Once we begin to think about the object of ministry, namely the world in which we are set, rather than how we can make our programmes successful, then our thinking becomes significantly different.

The call of leadership is to work with people to help nurture a passion and commitment to a particular geography around them. That is where they can cooperate with the Spirit in employing all of their God-given resources into that place to guarantee that in a specific time frame, every person will have had the opportunity to hear, understand, accept or reject the call to reconciliation with God the Father in the life, death and resurrection of Jesus the Son. We cannot build the church. Jesus and the Spirit do that. We cannot save people. The Spirit does that. But we as leaders can so envision, empower and release God's resources amongst Christ's people in such a way that the grace of God as expressed in the gospel is lived and declared in such a way that ALL of them can respond.

THE RECOVERY OF MISSION

The church begins to recover a sense of mission when it not only has a desire to share the gospel with as many people as possible but also when it begins actively to plan to make a difference in relation to a given circle of influence or account-ablity for which we are prepared to be held accountable to God and each other.

What is a circle of influence? The most obvious circles of personal influence are the people that we know well and with whom we have significant relationship. These could be family, friends, neighbours, colleagues at work, and those with whom we spend our leisure time. Many Christians have become used to the idea that we might invite people from our immediate circle of influence to attend an Alpha course or some similar encounter with Christianity. But that fails to address the question: what is the circle of influence that our church is responsible for?

In other words, what is the circle of influence that we want to encourage our church to explore and develop? Who are the people that our church desires to build relationships with, influence and reach with the gospel?

The most common response to such a question is usually defined geographically. Most churches have a strong sense of their given community. Churches that have a formal parish are rarely limited entirely to those boundaries. Churches which do not have a formal parish often recognise their informal parish boundaries, usually because the neighbourhood to which they relate has a strong sense of its own geographical identity. Most communities have physical boundaries shaped by major trunk roads, railway lines, canals, and the presence of factory estates, and amenities such as shops and schools.

The physicality of boundaries is qualified by two other factors. First, since at least the middle of the 20th century, far fewer people work within the communities in which they live. Increasingly, the most important personal relationships that people maintain outside of their immediate family cross geographical boundaries. Some churches have members with such strong relational networks that the geographical and community factors become significantly diminished.

Second, even when a geographical area does feature strongly in the call of a church, it may not be a call to everyone in that area. It is possible for some churches to have a particular call to an identifiable ethnic group or a particular age group or even a socio-economic group. A given church may be effective with some identifiable groups in a neighbourhood, but not with others. In such a situation, it is important to be realistic and also to ask, which other churches in our area can reach the people that we are unlikely to reach?

When a church wishes to take action in relation to mission, what kind of questions should a church be asking? What are action steps that need to be taken?

Step one therefore is to agree with your church the boundaries to which church relates.

Step two is to ask the far tougher question: do we accept responsibility for the community that we have identified?

Step three is to ask: are there other churches with whom we share this responsibility? Is it possible to build meaningful relationships with them so that we partner in the task?

Step four is to ask: how could we develop multiple opportunities to network with all of the people in our circle of influence for whom we accept responsibility?

Step five is to begin a planning process that includes measurable goals.

PLANNING TO INVADE SECULAR SPACE

In the previous chapter we talked about the fact that receptivity rises as the people of God talk regularly about the actions of God. It is possible to simply leave matters like that and see what happens. But there are other possibilities. Many churches in nations that are seeing a dramatic expansion of the kingdom are taking the natural and spontaneous passion of their people and helping them to be much more intentional in their encounter with secular people.

We are going to look at a specific case history taken from the Ukraine. Although there are some unusual circumstances in this situation emanating from the collapse of communism, it is important to remember that few would have anticipated the dramatic growth of the church 20 years ago. The expansion of the church has not been accidental. A number of key leaders chose to think strategically about the opportunities that lay before them.

A CASE STUDY

Immediately prior to the collapse of communism in Eastern Europe, few would have looked to the small Protestant community of the Ukraine for inspiration. Years of persecution and hardship had resulted in very slow growth. By 1990 there were approximately 1,000 Protestant congregations comprising Pentecostals, Baptists and many others, among a population of some fifty million. The historic form of Christianity had been Orthodoxy, and Protestants were viewed with suspicion. They were usually seen as a multiplicity of strange sects.

Yet today, approximately fifteen years after the collapse of the Berlin Wall, there are 7,500 congregations. There is a goal of planting 28,000 congregations by the year 2015. Why 28,000 congregations? Because church leaders in the Ukraine have calculated that this would be a sufficient number of congregations, strategically placed, for there to be a Protestant church within viable reach of everyone in the Ukraine. It is entirely possible that this goal will be reached. If so, the Ukraine could well be the first nation in Eastern Europe to have a majority Protestant population.

Some remarkable stories lie behind this explosive growth. Valerie Reshetinskiy leads Christian Hope Church in Kiev, a city of some 5,000,000 people. Valerie began his church with just six people in his living room in 1991. Today their congregation numbers more than 2,000. During this period they have planted more than 150 churches across the Ukraine, approximately half in Kiev itself.

Two key issues are important in terms of the case we have been making. First, the growth of Valerie's church and the church planting programme did not happen by accident. Both the growth of the mother church and the planting of new churches arose out of an intentional vision and planned activity. Second, although it is possible to argue that receptivity to the gospel has risen in the Ukraine, it certainly was not there to begin with. The collapse of communism gave rise to some degree of curiosity about new ideas, but there was no automatic interest in Christianity, especially in its Protestant form.

How did this growth take place? First, Valerie is someone with a vision, not just for the planting of a single church but for the evangelisation of a nation. That vision is represented on his wall by multiple maps. The first map is of Kiev, the second a map of the region, the third a map of the nation, and the fourth a map of the whole Russian-speaking world.

Second, Valerie has given substance to his vision through specific actions he has taken and values he has communicated. He has worked hard to build a leadership team in his own church which is deeply committed to the same vision and values. Valerie and the key leaders of Hope Church meet monthly. They revisit the vision, identify dates on the advance of the kingdom through them, resolve issues, and pray for God's strength and power. More than anything, these opportunities serve two important functions: to remind them why they exist and to ensure that they stay on track! Further, these meetings ensure accountability. Nobody is left out. Everyone is expected to be able to demonstrate what they have done to advance the kingdom of God in their particular circle. All are expected to report regularly on new church plants!

The same vision and values have been communicated to every member. This is critical, because the members translate the vision into action. The leaders "enable" the vision, but the members accomplish it together with the leaders. The leaders seek to create a ministry for every people group, geographical area and social need.

Third, Valerie and his leaders have worked hard to understand their context. They know their city and its needs. Following the collapse of communism, the Ukraine was devastated economically, religiously and sociologically. During the communist period, people had sufficient basic food to eat and the economy appeared stable for decades but under the surface all was not well. Abortion had become the birth control policy of choice by the government. Unwanted children existed on the margins of society. Divorce was commonplace, straining historically healthy family systems. Into this already fragile environment the freedom from the communism of the late 1980s brought chaos. Pensions disappeared. The currency, now competing with international currencies, was radically devalued. Economic hardship became widespread.

Many would look at a situation like this and conclude that the problems were so huge that there was nothing a resource-strapped church could do. However, over the next decade Valerie and his leaders developed specialised ministries to particular groups in mainstream culture, such as university students, the military and businessmen, as well as developing excellent ministries to society's marginalised and unprotected.

For older women whose husbands had died, and with pensions now nearly worthless, they developed a daily visitation scheme. The visitation teams listened, comforted, fed and provided medical care.

They reached out to tens of thousands of children living on the streets, occupied in glue sniffing and petty theft. They developed teams who go out onto the streets nightly. They find the children in every conceivable place where they can seek protection from the elements. The teams listen, comfort, feed, and provide medical attention. Where they can, they attempt to get the children off the streets. To support this, they have created a home where these children can move to. Once there, the children are clothed, educated and loved. In this environment the gospel of Jesus is declared and incarnated. They want to be the hands and feet of Jesus in order to give everyone an opportunity to respond to the gospel. The teams involve young people from the church giving out food, faith and love.

The upheaval of the last decade has left thousands of people on the edge of economic survival. To assist them, Hope Church has developed medical and dental clinics (some mobile). They distribute tons of clothing every year, and regularly feed as many as possible. It is important to stress that whenever they have begun these ministries they had first seen the need, then developed a vision with action. Only then did they pray in the physical resources to be able to address the need. Sometimes those resources have come into the country from elsewhere. For example, a great deal of medical help has come from Christians in Scandinavia. But little of that help would have arrived and less of it would have been effective without the activity generated by Hope Church. It is easier to give to an effective ministry than to a theoretical one that has not yet begun.

The fourth factor is the massive mobilisation of every member. The core conviction of each member is that they are ambassadors for God wherever they go. That ambassadorial function does not make them experts in every area of need, but it does make them willing to step outside of their comfort zone to pray for people and to expect God to act. Knowing that there are many in their church whom God has already freed from drugs, they are willing to pray for drug users, asking God to set them free. Seeing that God has changed the circumstances of many in their church, they have developed confidence to be able to pray for the needs of those they meet in their daily lives. To witness the active prayer of teenagers on the streets is to be deeply moved by their conviction in terms of the power of prayer in daily life.

This level of mobilisation is served through a cell-based system. As we have pointed out already, this practice, no matter what form the small groups take, provides a number of advantages. These revolve around the fact that the members of each small group see the needs of the neighbourhood very clearly indeed.

Because this model requires more leaders to make it function, the threshold for entry to leadership is lowered. The cell level of leadership demands less complex skills than those required to lead the whole church. The facilitator/leader of the small group is required to identify and train an assistant leader, ensuring future leaders for the expanding church.

Fifth, they have developed a training school for leaders and church planters. The training offers Bible knowledge but it also includes a highly practical element. The idea is to produce leaders who can translate knowledge into action. The training allows a very pragmatic approach to church planting. All possible thresholds are lowered, providing maximum resources to extend the gospel. They don't start with a building, so the cost of buying and building is eliminated. They don't start with a full-time person, so the costs of salary are lowered. They don't begin with an ordained leader, so seminary or Bible college graduates, with their expectations of pay and position, are counter-balanced. All new church plants are connected to regular training, accountability and problem solving. The key question is, "What do we need to do to plant a church?" Because leaders are constantly faced with human problems, they discuss them in such a way that the members respond, believing that God is calling their giftedness into action. So a new ministry begins.

This pragmatic approach to a divine mandate releases the full resources of the Spirit, and the full energies of people. When they pray, they know exactly what and who they are praying for. When the mixed gifts of people are put into strategies to initiate, harvest and consolidate, and invested into a particular place, they yield maximum results. If the new place has a significant number of alcoholics, then people gifted to touch, tell, provide medical help and harvest, are brought together. Many of these people will themselves be ex-alcoholics. If there are a significant number of street children, then people suitably gifted are commissioned to touch, tell, minister healing, and harvest in that field. Some will be former street children whom the church has already helped. Hope Church has been so successful with these ministries of social care that the government has sought to learn from their example.

This explosion of targeted resources has a significant impact, the cumulative result of which is the winning of people to Christ, the planting of a new church, the transformation of human hearts and the extension of the movement. The total impact of many people sharing their testimonies and offering practical help sharply increases receptivity to the gospel.

Sixth, the approach which has proved so effective in Kiev is being replicated in other key centres. This is accomplished by identifying key successful leaders who have the ability and the vision, not just to plant another church but to plant an "Antioch" or resource church in another key regional centre. They do this because they believe that they have a personal responsibility for the rest of the world. Valerie reminds us that when Jesus lived, God used the Roman Empire to pave 250,000 miles of primary and secondary roads, and to introduce a common language. He then asserts that God used the Russian government to do the same! He says that the Russians paved hundreds of thousands of miles of roads across the whole region, and superimposed one language, Russian, on the population. In his view, this was God's strategy to allow the Ukrainian church to take the gospel to every Russian speaking person and beyond – and, indeed the whole Ukrainian church has been active in sending out missionaries: some 1,000 Ukrainian missionaries have been sent in the last ten years to places outside the Ukraine.

We have turned the spotlight on Hope Church, and Valerie, but in truth, they are one of many like-minded churches in the Ukraine. God has ignited a movement in that nation. In the last few years many of the major denominations and church planting networks have launched what they call the "Antioch Church Movement" with the specific intention of evangelising the whole of the Ukraine and the Russian-speaking world. Along the way, they are asking God to make it possible for them to send 10,000 missionaries to the Russian-speaking world and beyond!

NOTES

1.   F F Bruce, *The Spreading Flame*, p. 95.

CHAPTER ELEVEN

LEADING A MOVEMENT

At its best, Christianity is a lay movement. Wherever Christianity is growing around the world, whether in South America, Asia, Africa or Eastern Europe, this single characteristic is the most significant element in that growth. That does not mean that there is no leadership, professional or volunteer, but it does mean that the goal of leadership is to empower and release the whole body of Christ in such a way that the creation of movement is the result. Mobilisation and multiplication, not attraction and addition, are the hallmarks of this kind of people movement.

But perhaps the most extraordinary aspect of these various people movements is that in many situations there was little sign of dramatic growth 30 or 40 years ago. More than this, if you had talked to any of the long-term leaders who were in the field a single generation ago, they would have reported to you that the work was hard, the people unreceptive and the churches lethargic. Few, if any, would have predicted the outbreak of movement.

That reality is bound to cause us to ask: what is it that causes the generation and growth of movement? Before we address this question, it is vital to be clear what we mean by movement. First, we are not talking about a transient fad or fashion that is here today and disappears tomorrow. Movements do have times of growth and decline, but we are talking about something which has a degree of longevity, that at least lasts beyond a single generation. Second, we are not describing a campaign or even a cause which is focussed around a single issue and which ends with the accomplishment of particular goals or outcomes.

Rather we are talking about a change in the way people look at the world, such that significant numbers of people are drawn to a passionate commitment to a cause, which is both significant enough to change their personal world and produce a determination to impact the whole world. Movements, especially spiritual movements, not only change a person's worldview but have a shaping energy sufficient to impact and change whole cultures. What then are the key stages in the development of movements?

1. The Divine Spark

Movements that impact whole cultures begin with individuals or small groups of people who are somehow transformed by a spiritual encounter that dramatically changes their personal lives. The occurrence of such encounters is probably more widespread than we sometimes imagine. Almost certainly, in every culture and generation some people have experiences of this kind. They cannot be planned for, predicted or arranged through a programme, but they almost certainly happen unexpectedly and spontaneously.

2. An Interpretative Framework

For a movement to develop out of such personal experiences it is necessary for someone to offer an explanation of these spiritual encounters to allow others to be part of that experience.

They may not themselves have the same experiences, but an interpretative framework can allow people to identify with those experiences. Peter did just that on the day of Pentecost. He did not say to the crowd, "This is just one of those things." Instead he explained that this is that which was promised in the prophecy of Joel. Having been offered such an explanation, and a clear way to identify with the experience, through belief in Jesus, repentance and baptism, others were able to join the movement, whether or not they had experienced exactly the same thing that had just taken place. Later, Peter did something of the same when the Holy Spirit descended on Gentiles. He offered an explanation, or interpretative framework, that allowed that new group of Gentiles to identify with the broader Christian movement. Movements are engendered when the initial participants begin to see a wider significance in that which they have experienced.

3. The Multiplication of Many

The capacity to mobilise people, such that the interpretive framework can be understood and explained by others, represents the moment of take-off for a movement. It is vital that movement is not dependent on the explanation of the experts or professionals. If it is, then multiplication is replaced by mere addition, and dynamic growth is not possible. Movements have to be highly transportable, and they are only transportable when every member can transmit the core explanation without help from an expert.

4. Power, Permanence and Purpose

Formal structures sometimes receive a bad press in relation to movements. There are many who see structure as the antithesis of movement. But in reality the creation of organisation actually adds power to the otherwise undirected energy of the initial movement. Of course, structures without creative energy do cause movements to plateau and then decline and it is often that phase of organisational life that people observe as the death knell of movement. But creative energy, well harnessed to organisational skill, represents the period of most rapid growth and impact for any movement.

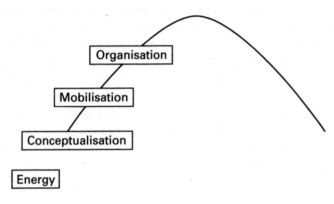

RECOVERING ROOTS

The implication of the above could be that it is always best to begin with nothing. Certainly there are those who are sufficiently disenchanted with existing structures that they simply do not have the heart or the vision or the will to renew that which already exists. That can be a matter of call and gift. Some are not called or able to renew existing structures, and have no alternative but to strike out afresh. But it is not inevitable for movements to ossify or to decline to the point of death. It is undeniably true that some movements or denominations are not renewed and do die. But there are sufficient examples of the renewal of movements to believe that decline and death are not inevitable outcomes.

We have paid attention above to what happens on the left hand side of the bell curve. It is also necessary to consider what might happen on the right hand side of the bell curve. Unless there is a significant intervention from gifted leadership, the usual pattern of movements or organisations features the following steps.

1. Plateau and the Beginning of Decline

There is a delicate balance required in the harnessing of creative energy to organisational skill. All too frequently, organisational skill will dominate over time at the expense of creative energy. As that takes place the watchword becomes "consolidation". In other words, the message goes out that we need a more stable organisation following a period of rapid growth so that gains are consolidated. That is a valid argument provided that the consolidation genuinely clears ground for another period of chaotic growth to take place. However, the likelihood is that the bringing of order signals that the creative people who disrupt order are no longer able to survive within the organisation and have already left.

2. Decline and Conflict

As decline sets in, organisations will generally polarise around two groups – the traditionalists and the radicals. These two groups have very different solutions to the problem of decline. The traditionalists wish to emphasise a return to the way we used to do things, believing that this will restore growth. The radicals emphasise the need to adopt new methods and solutions for a new day. They are both wrong.

3. Division and Death

Growing conflict will lead to some kind of division, with either the radicals or the conservatives departing. The outcome of such division is usually the death of the organisation. The death may be long and lingering or much more rapid, but in either case the organisation ceases to be effective in terms of its original life and vision.

The alternative scenario, difficult though it may be to achieve, is to attempt a process of renewal. Such processes can be accomplished at any point in the decline of an organisation, although clearly, the greater the decline, the more difficult the process of recovery. Renewal can come when creative leadership circumvents the conflict of traditionalists and radicals by asking a different question. The question that needs to be addressed is that of core purpose. Why was this organisation/ movement founded? What was its original genius? What was it that God entrusted to the initial participants? What was the Divine deposit that was originally gifted and can that be recast in the present context?

The recasting of the original Divine deposit in a new interpretative framework can allow a movement to be rekindled. Such a rekindling assumes a situation in which people are encountering God and coming to faith. If the new vision (interpretative framework) makes sense to these new believers and becomes once again transportable, then the movement can be reignited.

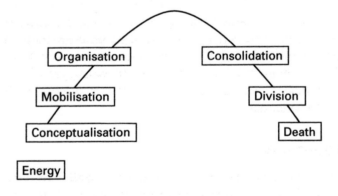

The rekindling of vision is an art more than a science but the following principles will help.

1. Be Realistic

Renewing organisations is hard work, and history and time tend to be against you. The renewal process requires the presence of creative people who are easily crushed by rigid structures and who tend not to have the patience for the long haul. You may need to protect some of these creative people by developing areas of experimentation where the normal rules of the organisation do not apply.

2. Spiritual Passion

The key issue at the beginning phase of renewal is not large numbers but passion and creativity. A small team with high levels of energy is worth much more than high levels of resource.

3. Look to the Margins

It is very rare for organisations to be renewed from the centre. If you happen to be at the centre, then look to the margins of your organisation for signs of life and nurture them. Give those on the margins permission, encouragement and legitimacy so that eventually the centre can be redefined in terms of the life that exists on the edge.

4. Live the Dream

It is vital to create the kind of teams that manifest in their working relationships something of the dream that they advocate. By living out what you seek to become, you establish healthy DNA for the future.

5. Spiritual Strength

The desire to do something different requires that leaders understand what they are up against. Organisations can have a life of their own, a personality that is bigger than the sum total of the individuals involved. Bringing change to organisations requires the spiritual strength to address that developed organisational personality.

6. Leadership is the Key

The recruitment and training of more leaders than you yourself can ever use is the key to the growth of movements. The lack of leadership development operates as the glass ceiling on the growth of every organisation. Developing innovative leadership training systems must be a high priority.

7. Kingdom Focus

The line between the kingdom of God and personal empire is all too fine a line on occasion. Keep a strong kingdom focus if you want to attract and keep those who have the capacity to generate movement.

8. Cheating History

To turn an organisation around so that it again becomes a movement is to cheat history. Be audacious enough to declare that this is what you are daring to do.

ACHIEVING MUCH WITHOUT THE MANY

The key to producing movement lies with the principle of multiplication. It is astonishing what can be produced from a very small initial base once multiplication is embedded in a movement. It is an observable reality that the world is constantly changed by committed minorities and not by apathetic majorities. The process by which small groups of people become mainstream influencers is well described in a book that describes the formation of secular movements, called *The Tipping Point: How Little Things Can Make a Big Difference* by Malcolm Gladwell.

The title of the book has begun to enter the vocabulary of politicians and social campaigners on both sides of the Atlantic. Although using very different words, the author describes the operation of key influencers that in Christian terms would be thought of as apostles and evangelists – those who cast the vision, build networks and then offer convincing advocacy. At a certain point, a new idea, ideology or even product reaches a tipping point such that it becomes the new orthodoxy. The many enter the scene at a fairly late stage in the process. It is the few that lay the groundwork to allow the many to enter later. The process of multiplication, or the production of a tipping point, has actually been given a mathematical formulation which Gladwell refers to in his book. He offers an astonishing illustration in relation to the developments of movements by citing a flu epidemic:

> Tipping Points are moments of great sensitivity. Changes made right at the Tipping Point can have enormous consequences. Our Canadian flu became an epidemic when the number of New Yorkers running into a flu carrier jumped from 50 to 55 a day. But had that same small change happened in the opposite direction, if the number had dropped from 50 to 45, that change would have pushed the number of flu victims down to 478 within a week. And within a few weeks more at that rate, the Canadian flu would have vanished from Manhattan entirely.[1]

Those kinds of statistics indicate precisely why movements need to become transportable in order to achieve significance.

Multiple contacts are vital elements in producing tipping points. The church planting teams that operate in the Ukraine are instructed to make 350 contacts each. They recognise that in terms of impact, large numbers of people must be contacted to produce initial momentum. It is precisely for that reason that church planting as an activity often becomes the point of leverage for the development of movement.

CHURCH PLANTING AND THE PRACTICE OF MULTIPLICATION

Church planting is taking place on a massive scale in some surprising places. Few in the Western world are aware that the number of churches in India has grown from 150,000 20 years ago to some 400,000 today. That vast expansion means that there are more churches in India today than in the United States of America.

However, it is easy to argue a case for church planting in a nation like India. The population is more than three times the size of the population of the United States of America and growing more rapidly. It is much more difficult to make a case for significant levels of church planting in the West because so many churches already exist. The cry goes up, how many new churches do we really need? If church planting is a necessary lever to produce movement and growth in our existing denominations, then surely it is a false hope, because with so many churches already in existence we can't all plant on a huge scale. It is all very well for small networks or denominations to church plant in an ambitious and even aggressive manner, but surely that is not a practical option for all of us?

These objections sound very conclusive, but before we simply bury church planting as a strategic lever for the generation of movement, we need to pause and consider. Three points need to be made.

First, throughout the centuries some churches do close either because they have run out of life or because the population pattern has changed. Shifts in the population mean that some church planting needs to take place simply to keep pace with these natural developments.

Second, church planting in a Western context does not necessarily mean the beginning of a completely new congregation as it might do in India or in other lands in the developing world. Church planting in the West might just as easily mean the replanting of a church that has severely declined. It could also mean the addition of other congregations or worship services within the same building to reach groups of people that the existing congregation cannot reach. It might mean the creation of new forms of church, either as cell groups, or home churches which only meet with other cells on an occasional basis.

Third, as we mentioned in chapter four, the basic disciplines of church planting are just as effective in terms of the renewal of existing congregations as they are for completely new congregations. The skills are entirely transferrable. It might even be the case that every minister who is planning to work in an existing congregation would benefit from a church planting course because the skills are very generic in terms of the growth of congregational life. That does not mean that every existing congregation either desires to grow or will easily accept the necessary changes that are implied in the growth process. Churches which are in severe decline and in need of help did not decline by accident! The evidence suggests that possibly a majority of churches which are in decline will not accept the changes necessary to bring renewal and growth. That is why so many have concluded that it is easier to church plant than to gear existing congregations towards growth. As many church planters comment, it is easier to have babies than raise the dead.

But given that church planting does look different in a Western context, that it can mean a more diverse range of activities, there is a case for networks of churches and denominations in the West to take another look at church planting, not just as another item on the agenda, but as a core denominational change strategy – transformative planting as we called it in chapter four.

What would transformative planting look like? In the first place it would require a huge investment of effort, if not money, in training. In 1992, during the Dawn Congress held in Birmingham, Peter Wagner, noting the goal of planting 20,000 churches by the year 2000, asked a difficult and disturbing question: "Where will you get 50,000 new leaders from?" Why 50,000 new leaders? In Wagner's view at that time, that is what it might take to plant 20,000 churches, or alternatively, we may argue, that is what it would take to change the church in Britain.

During the first half of the 1990s the conventional wisdom at Challenge 2000 (the body charged with encouraging church planting in the United Kingdom) believed that the Bible colleges would train all of the leaders that were required to fulfil the vision of 20,000 new churches by the year 2000. That was a forlorn hope. Bible colleges can only work with the candidates that they actually attract and the idea that 50,000 would offer themselves for full-time service was never really believed. In addition, Bible colleges have a duty to train more widely than the specific goal of church planting and so it was always unlikely that Bible colleges would be the route.

More importantly, it is at least open to question that formal training of professionals is the best route to produce church planters. The evidence from those parts of the world where church planting is proceeding apace suggests that non-formal training of those who will remain as lay people, or at most will become bi-vocational, represents the best avenue for the recruitment of church planters.

What would a training system that could train large numbers of people for the renewal of the church, such that students could study part-time and remain involved in leadership where they were, actually look like? That question is currently being addressed by many of the networks across the Western world that actually stand some chance of engaging in transformative church planting.

What is certain is that they will need to ensure that a certain kind of DNA, or convictions about multiplication, will be embedded in the training. Those convictions include at least the following:

1. An understanding that the purpose of the church is to allow the widest possible sharing of the grace of God with the whole community. In other words the purpose of the church is not to grow itself but to invade secular space with grace lived out in the lives of believers.
2. A conviction that the people of God have the potential to be mobilised and live in ways that make a difference. We have either expected too little of Christians or have expected that they will make a difference merely because they are exhorted through preaching to do so. If Christians are to fulfil their potential they will require a discipleship process that allows them to do what in any case they believe they should do but have never been shown how to do.
3. That kind of discipleship process can only be delivered by an approach to church leadership that is not looking first at hierarchical structures but at structures of empowerment. Church leadership must be careful not to perform activities on behalf of the people of God which it is the call of Christ for his people to engage in. In short, leadership should first and foremost empower the people of God, not be the people of God on their behalf.
4. In order to empower people, we have to trust people with activities that have normally been reserved for ordained leadership. That is how it was originally intended that the church should work. We see some small memories of that

original intention in the surprising fact that in the Roman Catholic Church, every Christian is, at least in theory if not in practice, permitted to baptise.

5. The empowering of people operates most effectively when people are encouraged to discover their gifts and use them. We should take some encouragement from the emergence in recent years of a variety of programmes designed to identify and release the gifts of every member.

6. Church leaders should use as their first measure of success the extent to which their people are mobilised, rather than how many people belong and attend. Numbers are not as important as the development of ministries amongst the membership. Few denominations ever ask such questions in annual returns.

Building into the life of the church these core multiplication values will lead to increased effectiveness. Increased numbers do not necessarily mean increased effectiveness. We must be careful not to be seduced by the numbers game. If denominations are serious about multiplication, then their strategies must include methodologies to engage in the following processes:

Coach the planting of a church or churches by themselves or with a team. This is still not the finest of Ephesians 4:11 ministry as Christ gave it, but it is the beginning of multiplication.

Coach churches that plant churches. This is not only the best use of the facilitative ministry of the Ephesians 4:11 functions; it is the fullness of multiplication and the beginning of movement.

Coach the denomination or network in such a way that the planting of churches that plant churches becomes a first order priority and not merely an additional programme amongst many. When this is achieved the fullness of movement can be anticipated.

Creative and highly motivated leaders who have built churches of large proportions, mainly in the West, have modelled entrepreneurial ideas about the church upon the church of our day. We have been seduced into thinking that this size impact is the same as effectiveness. In the face of this, God has raised up other, and even bigger churches, all over the world that bring these "success" criteria into question. These other churches are not so much successes of growth, but successes of growth and extension. They have extended the gospel throughout a people and place through the mobilisation of the full energies that God has placed within Christ's people.

Along the way, they have planted hundreds and thousands of churches, not simply programmatically, but as a result of the nature of the church in the world and as responsible before God for their place in his world.

We are not the first generation of Christians to see movement in our midst. Over the last several decades a number of nations have experienced what a number of us have called saturation church planting movements. Maybe one of the most encouraging examples of such a national movement has been the Philippines. In the early 1970s, through the vision and work of Jim Montgomery, many of the church leaders and denominations were galvanised by the Spirit to set their eyes on the full evangelisation of their nation in their lifetime. By the middle of the first decade, they had researched their context, visualised what the nation might look like if it were fully evangelised, and celebrated a national congress to motivate and mobilise the whole body of Christ towards this end.

Their research had revealed that by the year 2000 there would be nearly 50,000 neighbourhoods in which the population would be located. So, led by the Spirit, they set their hearts and prayers on seeing 50,000 churches planted by the year 2000. This would mean one church for every town, village and neighbourhood in every city by that time. Over the next two and a half decades the church leaders and para-church agencies conducted evangelism and planted churches with this vision in mind. By the year 2000 they had indeed seen God do through them what they believed he was asking them to do. Well over 40,000 new churches were planted and hundreds of thousands of new believers were born again into the kingdom of God![2] When a nation is reached through the extension of the gospel in such a manner, a number of factors can be seen to be working together, grounded in the DNA outlined in this book.

ASSUME RECEPTIVITY

It was this model of DAWN in the Philippines that originally inspired the organisation Challenge 2000 in the United Kingdom. That movement did not succeed and some argue that the reason for the lack of success lay in the absence of receptivity to the gospel. It was simply unrealistic for churches in the United Kingdom to obtain the spectacular results that had been obtained in the Philippines, a nation where belief in God was as natural as breathing air.

The issue of receptivity was undoubtedly a factor, but a much deeper issue lay in the fact that the DNA we describe above was present in the churches that were doing the planting in the Philippines. For the most part, it was not present in the churches that were active in planting in the United Kingdom. When that DNA is present in church, then, strangely, we can assume receptivity in the population, because, as we argued earlier, receptivity rises when the people of God speak continually about the actions of God.

Even without that reality, there is a great deal more receptivity in Western lands than we might suppose. We have argued earlier in this book that there is a growth of openness to spiritual matters in the Western world. We see that growth even in the secular writings of our time. The failure of the great alternative narrative to Christianity, the consumer narrative, is producing a deep ache in the hearts of many, so much so that

popular writers, academics and even the marketing professionals are picking up the deep sense of disenchantment or loss.
The American author, Zadie Smith, writing about American
life has suggested:

> Underneath the professional smiles there is a sadness that is sunk
> so deep in the culture that you can taste it in your morning
> Cheerios. It is internal and you can't sell anything to it . . .[3]

The business publication *Forbes Magazine* asked recently,
"Why are we so unhappy?" and they recruited a number of
international scholars to address the question. Their conclusion was, "We are a troubled civilization because of the loss of
a moral and spiritual center."[4]

Demos, the political think tank in Britain, commented in a
recent publication, "In the West we seek the good life, but we
have created an addictive culture that takes us further away
from it."[5] Even the marketing people are aware of the problem.
In a leading academic book on marketing, two writers make
this observation:

> For the first time in human history, a shared mythos has broken
> down, and commercial messages are now taking the place of
> shared sacred stories. We know in our hearts that a profession
> designed to sell products cannot fill this gap. If we take the time to
> think of how many people are finding the only meaning they have
> in their lives from consumption of various sorts, we do not feel
> proud; we feel sad, or even outraged.[6]

With feelings such as these commonplace in Western society, it
does not take much imagination to see why thousands are
seeking answers in strange places. Rob Frost, in a book that
seeks to critique the New Age Movement, quotes a source that
suggests that 27% of the population in Britain have successfully changed their spiritual life and a further 20% would like

to do so. [7] We are bound to ask what might happen if churches in the West were mobilised in the ways that we have described above.

Church renewal, saturation evangelism and church planting all conspire to cooperate with the Spirit of God to birth a movement in history when large numbers of people become followers of Jesus Christ in a short period of time. But it must be recognised that receptivity is a mystery of the work of the Holy Spirit influenced by human volition. No one can predict it nor fully explain why it happens. Such movements are seen in their fullness when receptivity is in place. This does not mean that the factors that describe and appear to cultivate and anticipate such movement are useless in places where there is as yet no demonstrable receptivity. Indeed, they instruct us that the kind of receptivity necessary to launch and celebrate the winning of the whole people or whole place will not come without these factors firmly in place. It is almost as if the very action of planning for a situation of receptivity seems to bring that very receptivity into being. We could almost argue that receptivity to the gospel always lies dormant until it is stimulated by the advent of determined activity.

As we have said so far in this book, the very nature of the church in the world predicates such expectation, while the actions of the people of Christ in the world are used by the Spirit of God to usher it in. When the church is acting like the church, and churches, motivated and envisioned, are winning people to Christ, and planting thousands of new churches, such multiplication will set the stage for the movement that we have prayed for. There are additional actions that we can take that further encourage the development of a movement that helps to facilitate receptivity.

First, movement and receptivity can be enhanced through the generation of exceptional unity, especially at a national level. That is not to say that movements do not happen without such unity, but the initial creation of movement is sufficiently difficult that examples of exceptional grace certainly help to create moments of openness for the Spirit to move. I say exceptional not because it is exceptional to God, but because it is exceptional to so much of our present reality. The preoccupation of local churches with their own life is multiplied in the denominations that they create and represent.

So many of us have succumbed to the idea of the church as the object of ministry rather than the church as the object of mobilisation, thinking that it is little wonder that we are unable to lever the kind of critical mass necessary to anticipate, create and harvest movement. Movement begins to come when churches and their denominations take on the biblical ideal of defining their existence not for themselves, their worship or teaching or programmes, but for the circle of accountability into which God has placed them and for which he will hold them accountable. When this happens, all of the resources that God has placed in them and are available to them are turned towards the target for which God has given them responsibility. It is only then that we begin to see the full impact of the DNA that God has created in Christ's people released with power on a people or place. Such intensity of resource investment, under and with the sovereign work of the Holy Spirit, creates what only God can create.

The second factor is active para-church cooperation. Encapsulated in the body of para-church organisations are many of the evangelistic, discipleship, caring and church planting gifts and strategies necessary to impact the circle of accountability. In and of themselves, the para-church organisations can make a significant impact for the gospel with their particular Spirit-given gifts. But, significant as these impacts may appear to be, they pale in comparison with what can happen when the whole body of Christ is released into the telling of their particular grace stories, using their particular grace gifts.

God did not design a small cadre of people, no matter how

gifted or motivated, to do what he has designed the whole to do. Not only do we lose the full impact of numbers of people when we fail to mobilise the whole; more importantly we lose the full impact and colour of the diversity contained in the whole of the body. A union of like gifts can make a significant impact, but it will never be as great as what the world will see when a significant portion of the whole paints the world with the full diversity of God's creation in Christ's people.

It is for these reasons that movement demands that para-church organisations and their gifts do not perform for or in the place of the church. Rather, they need to become active instruments in the hands of the Spirit of God to motivate, train and release the church into full effectiveness.

Third, movement demands that the church of Jesus be seen, heard and felt in the trenches of human experience. Transformational activity allows the love of God to be felt in all of the places where God, and pre-evangelism, needs it. Just as Wilberforce and the Clapham Sect sought to change the mind of a whole culture about the value of the church, the gospel and the Bible, so every movement needs to generate a degree of societal engagement such that needs are met and people are helped. That engagement can be at the level of working with children or addressing the problems of drugs, or mentoring young people. The possibilities are almost limitless. But whatever avenue or avenues are selected, they need to be audacious enough to make a significant difference.

Frontline Church in Liverpool wanted to begin a work amongst children, but whereas most churches would have settled for a group of 20 to 30 children and been pleased with it, Frontline have established a weekly programme that involves 1,500 children. The long-term societal impact of this work has been sufficient to rewrite the social history of a significant part of Liverpool. That impact has been noted by politicians, educationalists, social workers and most importantly by parents. The church has grown from an initial group of six visionaries to more than 800 people over a ten-year period.

Perhaps surprisingly, there is a great deal more of this kind of activity taking place than we might realise. Some research has suggested that in Great Britain there could be as many as 144,000 Christian projects in operation. (There is no eschatological significance in the figure 144,000!) Recently, the Christian organisation, Oasis, based in London, offered an award of £10,000 to the most impressive Christian social project. They placed details of the award on their website just to see what might happen. To their astonishment they received 194 applications in a very short period from projects whose total turnover came to some £23,250,000. Connecting such activity to a conscious endeavour to reach whole communities for Christ would significantly boost the impact of these projects.

Fourth, movement will require that the church aggressively, lovingly, but tenaciously tells the story of grace and the gospel to the whole of the people or place for which God has given them responsibility. This is the most obvious weakness in the churches of the West. We have stopped taking the gospel to our world in the sense of explaining the message. As we can see above, we are somewhat better at acting out the gospel than in explaining it. It is little wonder therefore that a time arrives when fewer and fewer people become Christians. The longer our lapse in broad-based, repeated and aggressive transmission of the gospel to the people in our world, the more difficult it will be when we do.

Even those who have an interest fostered by the ministry of the Holy Spirit will be easy prey to other forms of religious expression. Evangelists in some parts of Africa are very quick to remind Christians in Europe that it is not always the case that Africans are more receptive to the gospel than Europeans. But it is the case that African evangelists are far more persistent than their equivalents in many parts of Europe.

Some forms of such evangelism will demand the greater

cooperation that will come when the churches nationally are in greater visionary unity, and when the para-church organisations are cooperating with each other and empowering the church to do its work. This is true because some of the methods that we will use will demand more time, people and money than any one group can or should shoulder. I say "should" because even though at some levels one organisation might be able to "pull it off themselves", the message of God in his Son, Jesus, and in Christ's people, the church, is fuller and more effective when it is seen by the watching world as the expression of a much broader spectrum of church than any one group can possibly depict.

Fifth, we do need to think again about how we engender whole-nation movements such as we see in the Philippines. The apparent first-time failure of Challenge 2000 in the United Kingdom should not end our efforts. It is my personal experience, and I believe that it is the teaching that we see in the Bible, that facilitative teams need to operate at all levels of church life to assist the church to be empowered.[8]

What do we mean by such teams? In the Philippines, a national facilitative team was created to serve all the denominations. Ideally, national initiatives (or in the case of the United States at least state-wide initiatives) can have a significant impact on the generation of mobilisation. But it is also possible to generate regional, city or town-wide teams that work with every denomination and para-church agency to produce a strategic approach to the area that they have selected. There are some examples of a number of such city or regional initiatives beginning to emerge in both the United Kingdom and the United States.

Sixth, the generation of national movement requires a broad-based movement of local churches in the concert of prayer. This kind of prayer has already been referred to in a previous chapter, but its importance cannot be overemphasised. As the people of Christ begin to pray for the people for whom, and place for which, he has given them responsibility, God acts. But not only does God act; we begin to act as a response to God. It is impossible to pray for someone whom we see regularly and withhold a correspondent action. So, not only is God's untraceable sovereignty released, but his provision of witness and incarnation is equally released through Christ's people.

This book has been written in the expectation of such a reformation of thinking. The stimulation of our imagination can produce a situation where we do not wait for people to seek out our sacred space but where we begin to explore and invade secular space. The future is never decided by apathetic majorities, but by determined and courageous minorities. There are reasons for believing that Western culture is ready for such a movement of courage. There seems to be a longing at this time in Western culture for a new shared experience, a better way in which to order our world. A Christian people movement that can address such a longing will have powerful consequences for the evangelisation of our world.

NOTES

1. Malcolm Gladwell, *The Tipping Point: How Little Things Can Make a Big Difference*, Abacus, 2000, p. 261.
2. The full story of this amazing movement in our lifetime can be read in full in *The Discipling of a Nation* by Jim Montgomery and Donald McGavran, William Carey Publishers, 1980.
3. Zadie Smith, Foreword to Marco Cassini and Martina Testa, *The Buried Children of America*, Hamish Hamilton, 2003. Quoted in the Review section of *The Independent*, June 7th 2003.
4. Ravi Zacharias, *Can Man Live Without God?*, Word Publishing, 1994, p. 169.
5. Helena Wilkinson, Against the Addictive Society, *The*

Good Life, Demos Collection, 14, 1998, p. 83. (The author has contributed a chapter in a collection of essays.)

6. Margaret Mark and Carol S Pearson, *The Hero and the Outlaw*, McGraw-Hill, 2001, p. 359.
7. Rob Frost, *A Closer Look at New Age Spirituality*, Kingsway, 2001, p. 24.
8. More on this topic can be found in Dwight Smith's forthcoming book on leadership.

TOGETHER IN MISSION

Together in Mission is the successor body to Challenge 2000 which was established in the early 1990s with the goal of encouraging the denominations in Britain to take church planting seriously. The name was changed at the close of the 1990s because the original goals were tied to the year 2000.

Martin Robinson is the National Director of Together in Mission, and Dwight Smith works as part of the national team of Together in Mission. As an organisation, Together in Mission works primarily in the United Kingdom but offers training in other nations, and in partnership with Saturation Church Planting International works with a number of networks internationally.

Invading Secular Space explores concepts which Together in Mission seeks to implement with local churches, networks of churches in towns, areas and cities and with denominations. To that end a number of other resources are available.

M.A. in Missional Leadership

Together in Mission, working in partnership with Birmingham Christian College, has developed an M.A. in Missional Leadership. It is a part-time M.A. taught in local centres. The idea is to enable existing church leaders to study part-time without leaving employment and without having to travel long distances. The course is designed so that the concepts can be implemented in local leadership settings as they are learned. The application represents an important part of the learning process. If you would like to become a student or establish a local centre, please contact Together in Mission (address below).

B.Th. in Mission

If the M.A. is designed to equip existing leaders, the B.Th is designed to generate new leaders. The equipping of new leaders is essential if a church is to grow. Growing churches always train more leaders than they themselves can use. The B.Th should be available from September 2004 onwards. Enquiries should be sent to the address for Together in Mission below.

Introduction to Missional Church

Church leaders who wish to introduce their leadership to the core ideas contained in this book can use the Introduction to Missional Church as a simplified step-by-step study guide. Familiarity with the concepts will allow church leadership teams to think through how to implement missional thinking. Copies of this study guide cost £6.99 each or £49.00 for a pack of ten, available from Together in Mission.

Journey into Mission

Journey into Mission is a practical workbook which takes the key concepts and offers a route map for application of missional principles. Ideally a church leadership team will have a copy for every leader and will work with the manual to complete tasks and measure progress. These are available at £9.99 each, or £79.00 for a pack of ten books from Together in Mission.

Coaching for Church Planters

Together in Mission offers church planting coaching on a regional basis to small groups of practitioners in a seminar-style meeting on an agreed basis, either monthly or quarterly. At the meeting, the group will review progress, grapple with problems, and share encouragement and inspiration. If you would like to be part of such a group, contact Kevin Popely at Together in Mission.

Other Initiatives from Together in Mission

A range of other materials and initiatives are in the process of development and production. To keep informed you may wish to join the mailing list. Please contact Together in Mission to ask to be placed on the mailing list.

Together in Mission
Gold Hill Church
Gold Hill Common East
Chalfont St Peter
Bucks
SL9 9DG
UK

Or contact Kevin Popely personally on:
Tel: 01753 887173
E-mail: kevin@popely.fsnet.co.uk